INGREDIENTS OF CREATIVITY

ART SUPPLIES

MAKING, MANUFACTURING AND CREATING

BRUSHES BY GREENLEAF & BLUEBERRY

ENCYCLOPEDIA
OF
INSPIRATION

UPPERCASE

ART SUPPLIES

DESIGN

Janine Vangool

COPYEDITING

Correy Baldwin

UPPERCASE PUBLISHING INC

201B – 908, 17th Avenue SW
Calgary, Alberta, Canada T2T 0A3

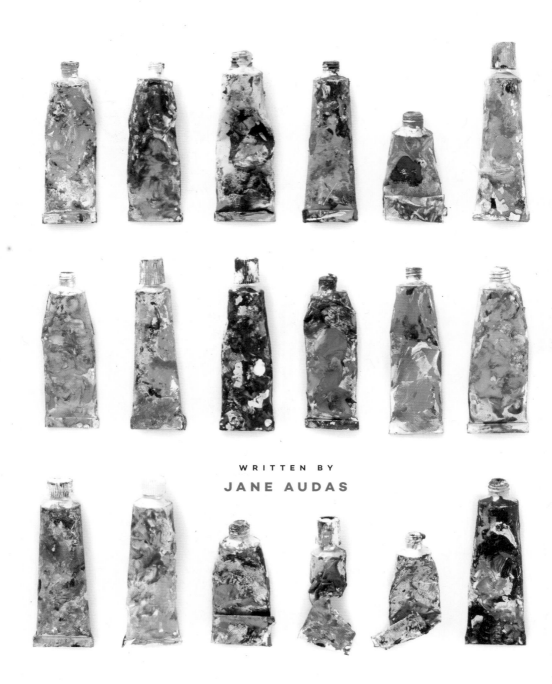

WRITTEN BY

JANE AUDAS

CONTENTS

TRACI BAUTISTA

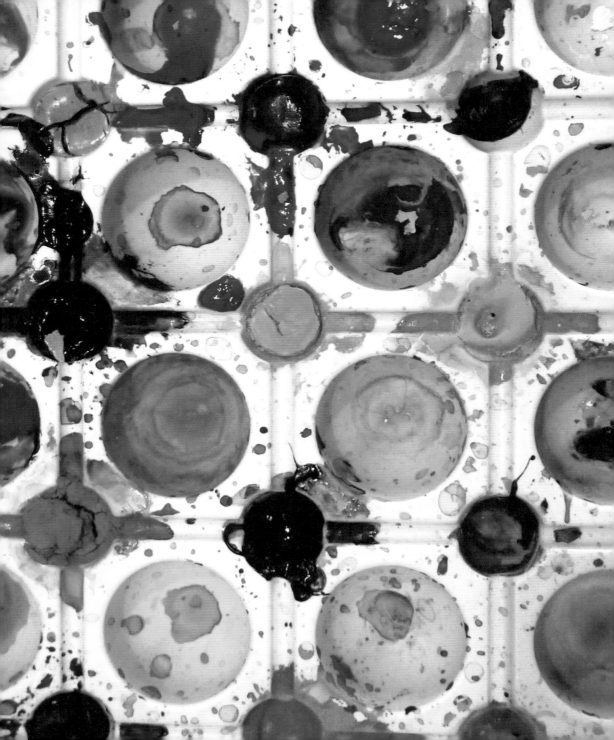

JENNIFER ORKIN LEWIS

Summer Sun Red

Cherry Magenta

Beach Rose

Wild Rose

Turtle Belly

Pumpkin

Bread

Morning Peach

Fall Poplar Yellow

ANDREW STEINBRECHER

A maker of graffiti-like prints and graphic quilts, Drew Steinbrecher works from his studio in Cincinnati, Ohio (watched over by his pet Schnauzer, Fred). Drew has been making for a long time: "I've enjoyed working with my hands and being creative from a young age. My dad was a doctor, which required excellent hand skills. I believe I inherited them, since I enjoy working with my hands. My mother has a great eye for design which I also inherited—a great combination for an artist!" Drew studied graphic design at university and "did the nine-to-five thing for over 10 years." Until one day, he walked into his boss' office and said, "I quit." He has been on his own ever since. "Which is way better," he says.

"I am a part-time artist, as I make half my living from my art and the other half from graphic design work." At a very basic level the two sides of his work and practice are the same: "The difference is the message. My design clients want me to convey their message, either literally or figuratively. With my art I get to convey my own message or thought." In his artistic pursuits, Drew began making quilts inspired by his monoprint and fabric collages: "I've always collaged, and quilt making is, in a way, a collage." The two sides of Drew's practice require completely different speeds of making; his quilts are thoughtful, time consuming—probably all-consuming—whilst his monoprints and collages are more intuitive and spontaneous, giving more instant artistic satisfaction.

Drew's training and skill as a graphic designer informs his art-making a great deal. In design school he

"I've always had the desire to create and be creative, so motivation as a maker comes easy to me. Of course, I know I have a voice and I am saying *something* with my art, but what exactly that thing *is* is difficult to put into words. I can tell you what inspires my art visually, but the *why* has always been a bit harder to find for me."

was trained in composition, colour, photography and visual problem-solving, and he found himself attracted to the graphic, bold nature of modern art quilts for their potential to frame a graphic of another kind: "A seam creates a hard edge which lends the medium to bold compositions." Collaging became a fast way to make studies in sketchbooks in-between making quilts: "I wanted to use my own collage papers, which led me to a gel plate, which has opened up a whole new world." A gel (or Gelli) plate is a clear, flexible surface on which you roll (or splash, or draw) paint. You then smooth each layer out with a small roller known as a brayer. Then, layering a piece of paper (or fabric) on top, you smooth it down and take a print off it.

Drew's studio is in the condo he shares with his boyfriend, Greg, in a building built in 1870: "We live in a very urban and historical neighbourhood called Over-the-Rhine. My studio is definitely crammed full

of stuff, but I know where everything is… mostly." Drew's print and collage work is definitively urban in feel—made from marks and layers of paint that give it a historical feel, reminiscent of layers of old peeling posters, where type and pattern are sometimes revealed, sometimes hidden: "Most people would describe my art as colourful and bold. I like strong graphic shapes. I use a lot of black in my work, which helps make the colour pop. I also like many layers, as it adds a richness and depth. Recently my art has been inspired by the controlled chaos and dichotomy of urban environments."

Drew has always felt more at home in the "hustle, bustle and crowds of cities," even though he calls himself an introvert: "Cities are controlled and regulated, yet they can be very chaotic and organic. Most cities are organized into 'blocks,' yet within these containers there are chaotic and contrasting urban elements, such as power lines, graffiti, nature, crumbling concrete, walls with torn posters, billboards, nature, wealth and poverty." Drew's work speaks to these words, too: his prints could be described as controlled yet chaotic, his quilts as regulated but organic. There is form to both of them, though. And that form is unapologetically and splendidly woven out of the urban visual chaos many of us live and work in. ❋

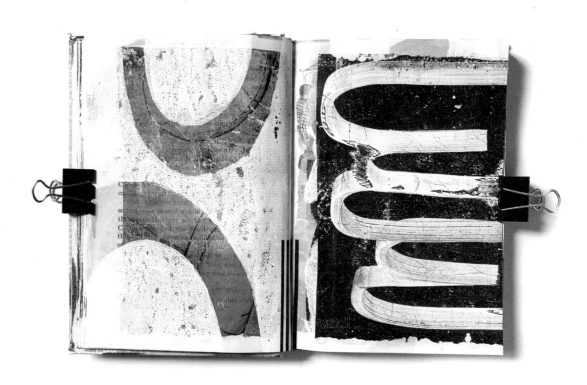

LAYERS OF MAKING

A gel plate is a soft gelatin-like plate that allows you to make monoprints using stencils, masks, stamps and other mark-making tools. You can make them yourself or buy them from manufacturers like Gelli Arts, whose plates Drew uses. Homemade ones don't last: "They need to be refrigerated and can get mouldy. It was a game-changer when Gelli Arts created a shelf-stable plate." Drew first discovered gel plates online: "I watched a YouTube video of an artist using one and thought it looked cool. I ordered one, tried it out and was addicted." He uses gel plates to make his collage papers; they give him a grungy look which he really likes.

For his collages Drew begins by making his collage papers on the gel plate: "I use acrylic paint in a variety of ways on the plate, along with stencils and tools for mark making. I print on a range of papers, from copy paper to tissue paper to vintage paper. I also use my own photography and gel print over the top, creating a layered effect." Once he has a selection he creates a collage in an altered vintage book or board book.

andrewsteinbrecher.com
@drewsteinbrecher

ARTFOAMIES

Most of us remember rubber stamps from our childhood art sessions. There was something so satisfying about the slight squish of paint under the stamp and watching how a fast-repeated image could quickly make up a pattern. Kae Pea, the owner and creative director of ArtFoamies, which makes foam art stamps, has had a passion for stamps for over 30 years—initially through her parents' company, Effie Glitzfinger's St. Louis Stamp Design, and then at RubberMoon Art Stamps, which she took over in 2012. Kae, who has a bachelor of fine arts in studio art from Maryville University, but also took graphic design classes, has now been at the helm of ArtFoamies since 2020. She has moved the business to her home town of Louisiana, Missouri, and now runs it with her husband, daughter and one other employee.

The stamps come in a wide variety of designs. As you might hope, there are lots of animals: birds, fish, cats, rabbits, dogs, a snail and even an elephant or two. All the holidays are included, from a Nordic-looking Christmas tree to Day of the Dead dancing skeletons. And there are moons and stars in heavenly abundance: "Our best-selling ArtFoamies are definitely those that lend themselves to mixed-media projects, things like backgrounds, abstract shapes, that can be incorporated into all kinds of different styles. They have the most mass appeal," says Kae.

Designs are by Kae and commissioned from a variety of artists, most of whom were already a part of the ArtFoamies and RubberMoon families. The

"We are small but mighty! We run the company with only two part-time employees (one of them being my daughter). My husband and I work full time, and occasionally we have a temporary helper for especially busy times. We do not have a physical store, but sell directly to art and craft supply stores around the world, including stores in Canada, Italy and the United States."

commissioned artist creates their image—sketching with pen on paper, or creating it digitally—and then Kae cleans up the image and converts the file into one that their machine can "read." She encourages her artists to design stamps they would use themselves: "My first piece of advice is for the artist to be true to themselves, their art and their voice—so I tell them to design ArtFoamies stamps that they would actually use and that they feel reflects their aesthetic."

Kae is keen to support her community with tutorials and recommendations. She publishes a lively blog with guest posts by artists showcasing the myriad of ways stamping can enhance art journaling, collage, fabric arts and more through layering, colour and patina. Since her business sells just the ArtFoamies, Kae has included a section on her website called KP's Faves, which includes links to paints, papers and brushes that pair well with her product. There is the delightfully named Super Sculpey Oven-Bake Clay, into which you can impress ArtFoamies designs to create more dimensional work. And, if you need help in loosening up and letting yourself experiment freely, she recommends the Buddist bestseller *Love for Imperfect Things: How to Accept Yourself in a World Striving for Perfection* by Haemin Sunim. ✳

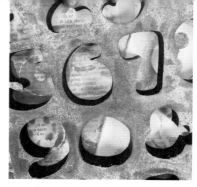

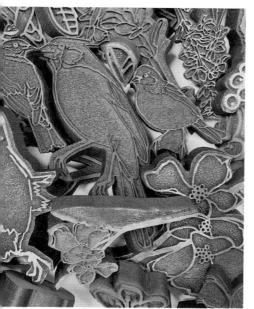

HOW TO USE ARTFOAMIES

An ArtFoamies stamp can be the main thing in the finished work, or a jumping-off point for making something bigger and more complex. With their many and varied designs, ArtFoamies supply a varied kit of parts that allow makers to, as Kae says: "add imagery to their artwork that they may not have been able or confident enough to make on their own." A blank piece of paper can be a scary thing and art supplies like these help lots of people discover the joy of making. Because ArtFoamies stamps are made of cushioned yet durable foam, they are a bit different from other art stamps (such as ones made of rubber or polymer) and they can be used with acrylic paint, fabric paint or inks to decorate most any surface that stays still long enough to be printed on, be it fabric, walls, floors, furniture, wood, curtains, tablecloths, scrapbook papers or gift wrap.

artfoamies.com
@artfoamies

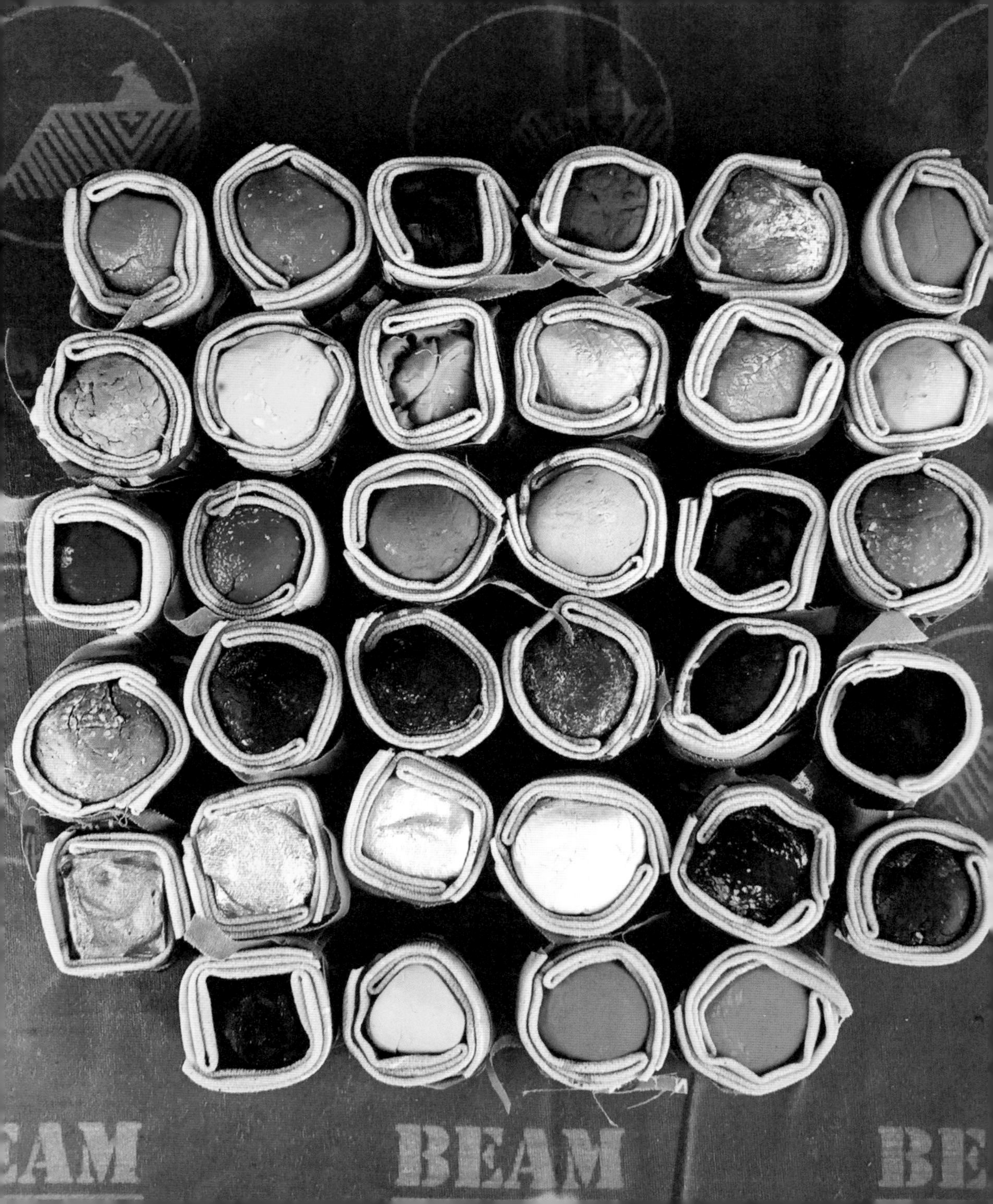
EAM
BEAM
BE

BEAM PAINTS

Anong Beam still lives in her parents' house—where she was taught to make paint by her father—in M'Chigeeng First Nation on Manitoulin Island, Canada. It is the most idyllic-looking place to make art supplies that you can imagine. Anong's farmhouse is made out of clay and earth, unusual for the area. The walls still have small drawings on them done by her father, artist Carl Beam. On site there is a good selection of out-houses and barns, and also a pheasant aviary, a little brown cow, chickens, goats (two babies with Monica, their mother) and lots of little birds. All Beam Paints and products are made and fulfilled from here. It is a self-sustaining place, as it needs to be, being so remote. Of course, living so remotely is not without issues, but the benefits are many.

Anong makes Beam Paints in her father's old studio building, which seems very appropriate: "Both my parents were artists and they had the thick skin to do that; it's very challenging. I did it for a number of years, where I was self-employed and I sold my work, took commissions and exhibited, so I had my experience of it. But I've always enjoyed business and people. I started a small art supply store selling watercolours and paintbrushes, as the island we live on has no art supply store."

But then everyone who came into the store had an expectation (and a hope) that Anong had made the paint herself: "And I realized I wanted to say: yes, I made the paint." Anong's (then) relationship fell apart and she found herself on her own, in her mother's

"I don't feel required as an Indigenous person to make everything out of what's just on the ground, willy-nilly. I feel like my contribution towards my culture comes from choosing to be a responsible, ethical producer, to make informed decisions—to make paint that is powerful but healthy."

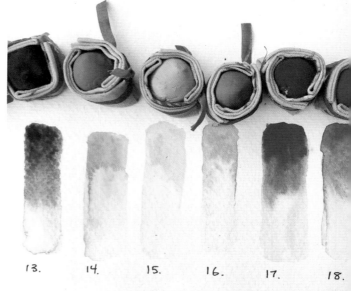

13. 14. 15. 16. 17. 18.

house, with her children. "We had nothing and I just decided to start making paint," she says. "It was the joy of feeling free. And it also took me back to my childhood with my parents, learning to make paint. I really used that to reconnect with my father and to bring that experience to share with my sons. It was a way to feel in love with my life and reconnect with people, because my father had passed away by then."

Her artist parents, Carl and Ann Beam, had been involved in traditional ceramic arts and had travelled to a lot of different Indigenous communities with a young Anong. Carl taught her to make Indigenous paints when she was small, and when she started making them again as an adult, the memory came back to her: "I had this moment of thinking: oh, I recognize you. I know what you are and how to do this. That was kind of a big moment for me. I started to share it and people were interested and I started a business. I had a full-time job at the time, working in a museum, and it was just a fun project to be able to talk about with people."

Beam watercolour paints are made from lush pigments blended with tree sap, gum arabic and Manitoulin honey. Not only do Beam Paints themselves please, they are also presented beautifully in palettes made from weathered cedar and pine branches from the forest floor, carved into mini, half pan and full pan holders: "I couldn't take that paint I was making and put it in plastic half pans; it was just something so organic and real. The love of the material was so strong for me and when I put it into the plastic, it didn't fit. My partner runs an Indigenous forestry and lumber sawmill and there are little pieces of wood everywhere. And they suggested themselves to be used."

Beam Paints sells collections of colours—Mother Earth Palettes, Cedar Forest Colours, Love Paints and Great Lakes, to name a few. The watercolour paints look like jewels set into their wooden palettes. All the

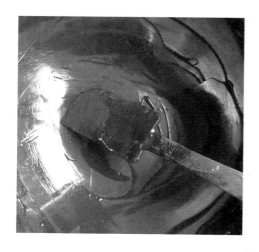

M'skwi Inaatig'aande
Red Maple Colour

Awun'aande
(Fog colour)
GREY OCHRE

Zhiibiigeh'Aazhibik
aande
SLATE
(writing stone colour)

Ngwankwat
GREY ULTRA
(cloud)

Mkwumi'aande
ice colour
(gouache)

Waaskonense
Violet
(flower)

Zhoomin'ande
Grape

Gaatchi Waaskonense
aande
Lavender
(small flower colour)

Dwaagi Aadzibuk'aande
Fall Poplar Yellow

Strange Bay
(Lakebed)

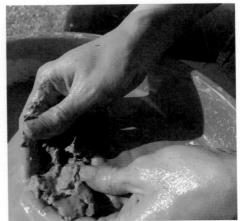

colours are named in Anong's native Ojibwe language: Wiigwaasmin'aande is a (hot pink) cherry magenta colour, Kosmaan'aande is a (sun-drenched orange) pumpkin colour, and Shingwauk'aande is a (fresh, rain-drenched green) pine colour. Some of the colours are particularly local: "I have a paint called Strange Bay. We had set anchor in a bay whilst fishing. When we pulled up the anchor the muck on the bottom was this beautiful kind of French grey. We had to stay in that bay because the wind had blown up and there was a lot of stormy weather. So my sons and I spent the afternoon just diving and gathering the muck. And we made paint from it. We named it after the bay, which was called Strange Bay."

"We have some local stone that is in all of our paint mixes. I think that's what gives our paints an earthier feel. People report that they like the brush feel of them— they're a little different."

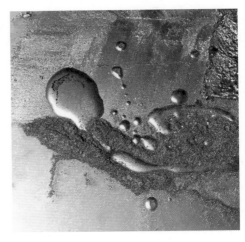

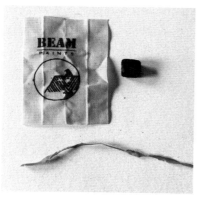

When she started Beam Paints, Anong made everything herself. She now employs 11 people, full time and part time. Because of their location they were able to offer people homeworking even before the pandemic. "That gave us the ability to give work to young mothers and disabled people," she says. "That was really important to me because most of the work around here is very strenuous and the best paying work is for fit men. So it felt really good to me to be able to offer something to people who were needing that kind of support. Right now, a significant amount of our paints are wrapped by a Mennonite family and also a man who's recovering from brain surgery. He is unable to go to his former work. He finds doing this kind of work is very therapeutic for him." They also support different local beekeepers (and keep bees themselves) and use the wax to finish off all the palettes.

Maudji Nmehgonse
Wild Salmon

"When I make paint I think about my dad a lot. He taught me when I was really small to identify hematite and look for paintstones. He kept them in his art bag in a little cloth wrapper, and when he needed paint he brought them out and prepared his paint for ceramic bowls, drums or rocks."

"This is me in a pot made with hand-dug clay and painted with foraged pigments from North America. I was really fortunate to be raised by artists Ann and Carl Beam, and as a homeschool kid I travelled the continent with them gathering rocks, crystals and generally investigating. I am happy to be doing the same many years later with my own sons."

A WORD FOR ARTIST

In our culture there isn't really a word for artist; it's more connected with being a shamanic (or spiritual) person. There was so much power associated with making an image and my father [Carl Beam, 1943–2005] was interested in those sorts of things. Historically the act of making pigments, and also working with ceramics, has really been taken away from us as a people, because the historical artefacts of our own paint making and ceramics, and our earth practice, had been collected by anthropologists and then removed to storage. But in the locations where they store them they don't show them or talk about them. In my father's time it was really common for people to say: no, we don't do that, or that's not traditional. The knowledge was on the edge of being lost. He travelled to a lot of different places and learned from a lot of Indigenous practitioners about pigments and paints. That was his passion.

Although Anong does still paint, she keeps her paintings quite private: "I never felt the drive that my parents felt to make painting my everything. Instead, it became everything to me in another way. I've always really enjoyed other people's art. For me, it is really enjoyable to see what other people are doing, because there are so many other people doing so many different things, more than I could ever imagine doing in my small life. It's very fine to see all of that and to be a part of it." ✳

Summer Sunset

Cherry Magenta

Beach Rose

Wild Rose

Turtle belly

Pumpkin

Bread

Morning Peach

Fall Poplar Yellow

Harvest Wheat

Butter

Cloudless Sulphur

Milkweed

Spring Green

Pine Green

Salish Sea

Boreal

Lake Huron Teal

Ice Blue

Great Ocean

Prussian Blue

Almost Night

CERTIFIED ART SUPPLIES

Anong Beam is aware that the use of the word "natural" today always makes people think something is automatically non-toxic and good for them, and for the environment. "I think that artists aren't really aware of the fact that in art supplies, it's almost the opposite: that natural colours—quite a few of the ones that make bright hues—are very toxic," she says. Anong takes the responsibility of producing non-toxic pigment paints very seriously: "I think people assume that everything that I use is natural. I try to be very upfront with the fact that I am looking to make the best paint, period. And that means that I use synthetic pigments. I'm very, very choosy about what we use."

Beam Paints has joined the Art and Creative Materials Institute (ACMI): "In my opinion, ethically responsible producers belong to that society because they have stringent toxicological requirements. We have 27 of our colours currently approved by the ACMI. It was really good for me to do that. It's been tedious. It's pricey. And I think we are the smallest manufacturer that they work with. But they've been very generous with their time to help us achieve that AP (Approved Product) certification."

Slate

"I'm an artist and I appreciate the full range of colour. It was important to me to make paints— all the colours of paint."

beampaints.com
@beampaints

BELINDA DEL PESCO

Coming to art later in life sometimes makes for a more intensive, lively practice. Printmaker and water-colour painter Belinda Del Pesco seems to be redefining keeping busy while making up decades of lost time spent in uncreative jobs: "I started making art after a long hiatus filled with jobs and family, so I'm a late bloomer. But the delayed start added urgency to my curiosity and drive."

An active blogger since 2005, Belinda has shared her creative journey online and nurtured the mono-type and collagraph printmaking community through her website, YouTube channel and courses. "While working in a non-art career, I'd been absent from creative pursuits for many years," she says. "Blog-ging about my timid first steps, and sharing the var-ious art-making methods I was experimenting with brought comments from other artists—both active and on hiatus. That new community helped balance alone time in the studio. And the volley of communi-cation and shared links exposed my wondering to all sorts of new venues, art groups, publications, shows and ideas. Blogging has been a deep well of resources, friendships, marketing ideas, art sales and verbal ex-pression related to being an artist."

Her artworks—paintings, drypoints, monotypes, collagraphs, linocuts and woodcuts—all have subjects centred in the domestic in common. Belinda prefers to paint and print subjects that are, physically and emotionally, close to her: "My art is inspired by im-ages of my family and the rooms we live in, snapped surreptitiously with my cell phone. I also use vintage

"When I've got art supplies in my hands, I'm still, calm, focused and happy. I don't sense time, chaos or worries. Art-making is the most potent and natural atmospheric adjustment tool I know."

family photos taken many years ago." And her themes are closely tied to her materials: reused and upcycled found domestic flotsam. Her "plates" for her etchings might be the side of a tissue or ice cream box, with unusual dimensions, utilitarian colours and odd finishes on the cardboard. One might be used for an etching of a cat; another for a bowl of limes. The clear plastic inside tomato packaging might be used for an etching of a child in a plastic paddling pool. "I've had a lot of fun printing drypoints from plastic produce boxes and collagraph prints from box-card pantry and frozen food containers, or foil-lined soup boxes," she says. "The materials are readily available in our refrigerators and cupboards, and using them to create art gives recyclables new life."

But it all starts with "noticing," with Belinda taking a snap on her mobile phone and printing the photo as a reference: "Then I start drawing. Sometimes, I combine several images as a composite. I make notes in the margins as colour or design elements occur to me while I sketch. After the drawing is finished, I either paint the scene in watercolours, or begin carving the plate (mat board, plexiglass, cardboard, plastic, lino or wood). While working, I listen to audiobooks and podcasts. After the plate is prepared, I tear paper down to make a small edition. I mix printmaking ink, and pull-down sample colours in a notebook with details on the ingredients jotted in the margins. Then I begin printing."

The fact that Belinda's materials are not precious or expensive frees her up. "Using materials you would otherwise toss encourages a bit of whimsy in the making," she says. "You didn't *buy* the plate you're incising from an art supplier, so you have permission to use freer lines and experimental design ideas, without worrying about messing up or wasting purchased art supplies. If you make a mistake, grin and shoulder shrug, and then snip another cracker box to make a new plate."

Belinda's final prints carry the memory of the original materials too; often a softened line results from using her found material "plates." She also often hand-colours the monotone prints, lending them a romantic, blurry air that complements the subject matter. There is a tension, a soft ying and yang, between her etched lines and gentle colours: "My favourite themes are unposed figures, reading, hanging out together, working with their hands, napping, etc. I also love creating tilted, close-up compositions of still-life

scenes, or flowers in glass vases reflected on glossy tiles, sunny room interiors and occasional landscapes. I make art that sneaks custody of the quiet, intimate seconds in between the flurry of day-to-day hours. Painting and printing items, rooms and moments of interaction that seem unremarkable, in a way that makes them more fetching, is very satisfying."

The thrill (and comfort) of the everyday is in all of Belinda's work, where unremarkable art supply materials meet "unremarkable" domestic subjects. The results are much more than the sum of their parts. ✳

"I'm very fortunate to always feel inspired. Perhaps because I started taking art seriously a bit late, I feel there's no time to be blocked or frivolous about my time to make art. Life can still occupy too much of my art-making time, but I return to creativity over and over again like a thirsty person gulping water."

belindadelpesco.com
@bdelpesco

B. DEL PESCO

A ROOM OF ONE'S OWN

Belinda's studio is a small room in her house, with a window curtained from the outside by leaves of an old macadamia nut tree. Her worktable faces the window, covered with plexiglass for ink mixing. It has been adjusted to standing height with lifts under each leg. Short bookcases flank it on each side, filled with watercolour and printmaking books, a postal scale for weighing outbound art and bins of printmaking ink. Her Takach etching press lines the wall to the right. The shelving underneath the press stores paper, linoleum and wood for relief prints. On the wall near the door behind where she sits, a large sheet of building insulation is used as a pin-nable easel for watercolours in process. Baker's racks are in a closet, lined with bins of carving tools, shipping and framing supplies, video equipment and rescued sheets of plastic and card-board from food containers to make prints. Unframed art inventory listed in her Etsy shop are filed upright in baskets, sorted alphabet-ically. A length of paracord is suspended between eye-hooks across the room for print drying purposes.

CALLEN SCHAUB

I f you have seen Callen Schaub make art on Instagram—and with over 700-thousand followers, the chances are good you have come across him—you will know his process can involve pulleys, spinning canvases, copious amounts of poured acrylic paint and sometimes a moving artist, too. It is an extraordinary performance to watch.

He has found his own unconventional path to success, one that plays to his strengths as an unconventional artist: "Being a non-traditional painter, it took several years and a lot of criticism from members of the fine arts community and the Internet before I was able to block out the negativity and lean into my success. Having a presence on social media and sharing my art on those platforms was a huge part of my creative path. It presented a global stage, if you will, to share my art and positive messaging with an audience that I wouldn't have had access to, had I just exhibited in Toronto." On social media Callen often posts performative films that give insight into his process—part physical performance, part DIY project—but that are also exciting to watch—pulling in non-traditional art audiences who otherwise might not see art in traditional gallery spaces.

Callen's mother was an artist and he grew up comfortable around paint, art and creativity. He attended high school at the Etobicoke School of the Arts in Toronto, where he first started experimenting with abstract art. That was followed by a degree at the Ontario College of Art and Design, "where I fully dove into spin painting and developed the apparatus and tools that help me create the styles of art I am known for today,"

"Every day is an opportunity to make the world a little bit more colourful, and I feel very grateful to be able to do what I love and share my vision while connecting with other people on such a large scale. I get to wake up and create art with the person I love and share it with a community of people whose stories I am inspired by. What could be better than that?"

he says. Callen ran an art gallery for several years after graduating and has been exhibiting his abstract spin paintings and performing live spin paintings since 2011. In the years since then he has perfected the art of showmanship and self-promotion and has found the Internet to be a perfect outlet for his artist "brand."

Callen's studio in Montreal is an extension, if not a visualization, of his process: "I work in a large paint-splattered warehouse in Montreal, Quebec, Canada. Large inventories of paint cans are stacked up against the walls in the warehouse and canvases are being delivered and shipped out in crates at a rapid rate. Photoshoots, project builds and drying paintings take up much of the otherwise open space. It's controlled chaos with tools, ladders, tripods and wet paint everywhere. It's heaven."

His "mad inventor" approach to art supply tools began in college, where Callen first began doing his spin paintings using a potter's wheel. He then moved on to a repurposed, rewelded bicycle crank: "My favourite tool, and also the one I use consistently, is the

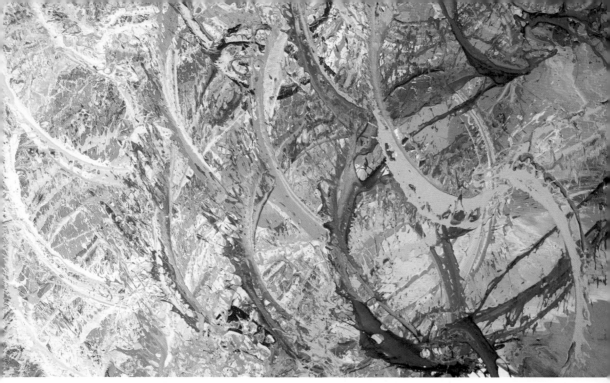

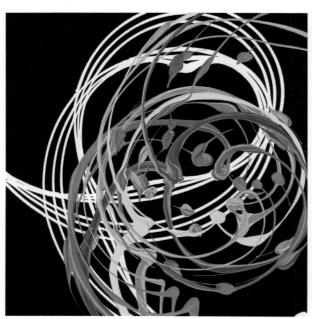

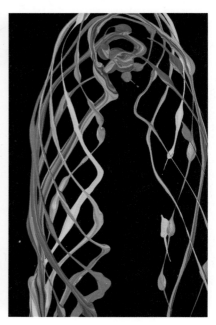

NO ORDINARY PROCESS

Before he begins painting, Callen works with his collaborator and partner, Sparkles, to design the colour palette for the forthcoming work. They consult on style, approach, techniques and canvas before he spends time setting up the tools and apparatuses required: "Once the preliminary setup is complete it is important that I focus on creating a judgement-free headspace, so I can create in a positive mental space. I take a few deep breaths and turn on all the cameras." All his work is recorded on video and often simultaneously broadcast live on social media. "As I begin the process of painting, the performance of creating also begins. I start by pouring large quantities of acrylic paint into the centre of the horizontal canvas that is mounted onto what I call the "Spinner," which is the retrofitted bicycle I use to spin my canvases. I then manipulate the paint with various palette knives. Then I spin the canvas until the paint reaches the edges of the canvas. I then load the trapeze or bucket full of colour, then deploy it and let it swing over the spinning canvas to capture the effusion of colours and motion." Then the artwork is complete.

spinner that I created from an old bike. My warehouse houses my mobile studio, which I call the Arena, which is a circular splash zone 12 feet in diameter and 3 feet tall. Above the Arena, various paint trapezes and pendulums are strung up to the ceiling. This is where the mess and magic happen." His paintings are created with fluid acrylic, his paint of choice, on a gessoed canvas or panel.

Callen's art is about nothing if not colour; after you get over watching his proces, it is his defining trademark: "The use of colour is how I reflect my personality in my work. I am a happy and positive guy, and I try to create works of art that evoke joy in others. The beauty of abstract art is it can be interpreted however you want, and what makes it beautiful is fully in the eye of the beholder. Basically, when it comes to abstract art there are no wrong answers, and that's what I love about it." He has been open about how his art has helped him with his mental health, that making art made him feel better: "The initial motivating factor for me when I started my career as an artist was simply that it made me feel good, and was great for my mental health. Being candid about that on the Internet opened up a lot of really wonderful conversations with other people who shared their stories about their struggles with mental health. What started as me making art to make *me* feel good, turned into something much bigger than that." ✳

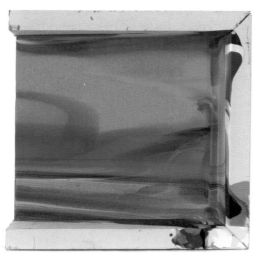

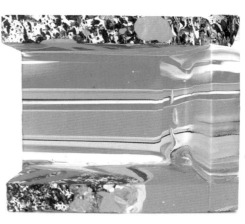

INCIDENTAL ART

"The nature of the kind of art I do does contribute to a certain level of waste, but we make the best attempt we can to create art from the wasted paint—which is what spawned my confetti pop method. By lining the painting arena with blank canvasses, we are able to collect the spray from the active canvas and turn it into another piece of art. The floor is also lined with canvases that then become incidental finished artworks as well. Even my paint-covered clothes I sell as fine art. I have now been collecting used paint cans, jugs and cups to be repurposed into sculptures as well. I'm always looking for new ways to turn all aspects of my practice into finished pieces of art, not waste."

INDUSTRIAL AMOUNTS OF PAINT

Making a Callen Schaub painting is no simple undertaking. Aside from the engineering and builds of his unique techniques, he uses a lot of art supply materials. The amount of paint he uses is determined by the finished scale of each painting but can be between one to two litres and five to ten gallons—annually he uses an impressive 250 gallons of paint. For each painting he will spend anywhere between $60 to $400 on a canvas and then an additional $100 to $500 on paint, depending on the complexity of the project. The majority of that cost is borne by Callen himself, but sometimes he receives sponsorship: "I do have brand partnerships with Tri-Art, where they give me a discount when I post about their product. And Art Resin gives me a set amount of free resin per month in exchange for posting. I also get a discount from Faux Cadres when I post." He doesn't order a specific set of "favourite" paint colours every time, as he likes to experiment: "I love to explore the emotional effects of the full spectrum of colours, so I try to keep a full inventory of every colour of the rainbow. That being said, I tend to gravitate towards brighter colours, as they show up better on the canvas."

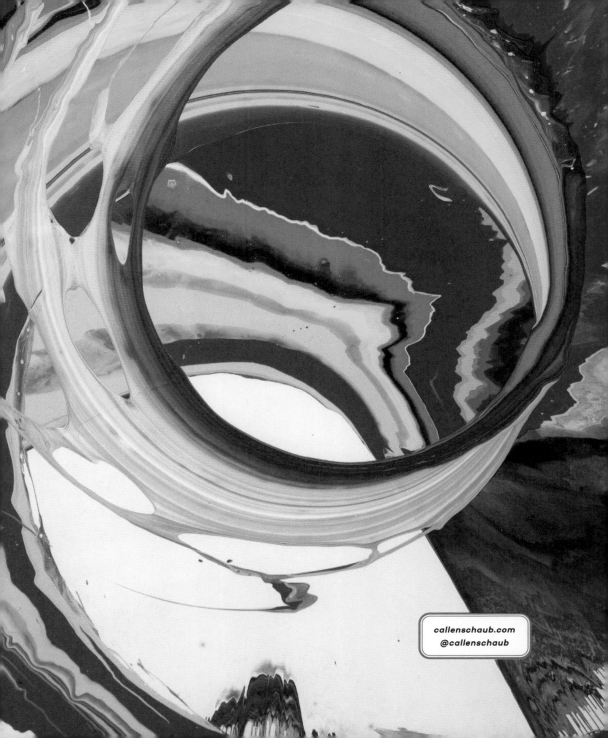

CHALK COPENHAGEN

Chalk is a naturally occurring material—and one of our earliest art supplies, used as far back as the Paleolithic period, when drawings in caves were made with ground pigments mixed with spit or animal fat and applied as a paste or as a spray paint blown through hollow bones. Chalk comes in three natural shades: white, red and black. White chalk is made from limestone, itself created from crushed shells of microscopic marine algae. Red chalk is made from an iron-oxide pigment-containing clay, and black chalk is made from shale, a nice concoction of black and grey minerals.

Chalk was traditionally used as a sketching medium for making drawings, very much seen as a preparatory medium before painting. In 16th-century Italy, travelling artists used chalk to draw Madonnas on pavements; Michelangelo also used it, although he could afford paper. Chalks did not really come to the surface until the late 19th century, when Impressionist artists like Pissarro saw the potential in chalks for making finished artwork. So, although chalk-making may be a new endeavour for Conny Viès and Lene Zerakitsky Andersen, two sisters in Copenhagen, they are making a centuries-old art supply. In fact, many of the pigments they use are the same ones that have been used by artists for centuries.

Chalk Copenhagen is based in the village of Højerup on the beautiful limestone cliffs of Stevns Klint, in Denmark, a UNESCO site of geographical importance. It is where Conny and Lene were born and brought up. The chalks are made in simple rooms

"Our pastel chalks are used by professional artists, architects, designers, students and others with an interest in art and sustainability."

here, with a view over the white cliffs, the sea and the fields. "It is in these scenic surroundings and with the raw materials of nature that we shape the sustainable pastel chalks," they say. "It was the idea of creating sustainable artist materials from the local chalk that made us start this project."

Chalk Copenhagen's manufacturing processes are based on old craft traditions but they are constantly thinking of environmentally sustainable solutions. They can be confident in what they are making and how because they are a small company, with their hands on every part of the business: "We develop the recipes ourselves, mix and match the colours, knead, roll, dry, cut and pack the chalk to finally sending them out into the world." There is a very high content of colour pigments in their pastel chalks and the colour pigments can easily be mixed and blended together. The chalks come in luscious but gentle colours "from the areas of the world where the most beautiful shades occur," and are all mixed by hand to create colour combinations that are close to nature and the Nordic light that Conny and Lene see outside their window: "We produce the pastel chalks with lightfast natural earth tones, plant colours and iron oxides. We primarily use earth tones and iron oxides. Mostly we buy ready-made but some pigments we clean, decant and tear ourselves. We mix the binders from natural materials, and neither our pastel chalks nor our fixatives contain plastic. We do not add preservatives or other substances that may have endocrine-disrupting or carcinogenic effects." And the beautiful boxes that the chalks come in are equally

"It is our goal that with our products we can make a difference for each user's experience and creative expression and at the same time take care of the environment."

thoughtful. Each wooden box has its own history, recycled from part of a coffee table, a window frame, a floorboard or something completely different.

Chalk Copenhagen makes a small but beautifully formed product. The passion of its owners is squeezed into every small box. The only time the sisters have been tempted to make something different was when they made an exclusive set of chalks in collaboration with specialists at the Skagens Museum in Denmark. Those chalks were based on the luminous paintings of Anna Ancher (1859–1935) and were commissioned to accompany a large retrospective exhibition of her work. Ancher was a woman artist considered to be one of the country's greatest painters. "We analyzed her paintings and looked at the colours in her old paint boxes that contained a number of different pastel chalks," they say. You can only buy these particular Chalk Copenhagen pastels in the museum shop in Skagen. It is a lovely excuse to visit! ✳

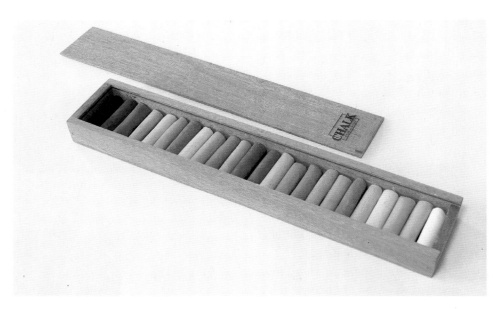

Chalk Copenhagen makes their pastel chalk from pure chalk from Stevns (the cliffs) and uses only natural binders. They colour the pastel chalks with natural earth tones, plant colours and iron oxides. "Natural pigments are found in many different places in the world, but there are not many who trade them, as synthetic pigments are gradually dominating the market," the company says. "The temperature is crucial for the colour and glow of the pigment. When burning at 700 to 800 degrees, for instance, yellow ocher turns to red and if the same pigment is burned at higher temperatures, the colour becomes a cool brown-violet like caput mortuum."

Earth colours vary depending on the area in which they are dug up: "The brown umbra from Italy is relatively light compared to the almost black umbra from Cyprus." With this in mind, Chalk Copenhagen uses the Danish leaf shell ochre, specifically from the small town of Løvskal, where there was once an ochre factory: "If you dig a little into the ground, you can still find the beautiful ochre."

At the workshop in Højerup, they combine chalk with binders from natural materials, knead the chalk mass in a large industrial mixer and then roll each cylinder by hand before drying. Finally, the chalks are cut into lengths before being carefully packed in boxes.

chalkcph.com
@chalkcopenhagen

CHRISTI YORK

After a formal training in graphic design, Christi York spent 20 years or so doing graphics, alongside making accessories and jewellery. Then about five years ago she began making her "art from nature" full time. She now makes sculptural basketry, botanical prints and handmade ink and paints: "The minute I found out I could create something with 'cast-off' plant materials, it was an 'ah ha' moment; it became *all* about the material being my inspiration source. For me, the material *is* the muse. I make sculptural basketry pieces out of natural plant material that I harvest and process myself. I create my own watercolour paint out of foraged pigment rocks and I make ink out of flower petals. Since the pandemic, I've also taken a deep dive into botanical eco printing on paper." She heard the call of natural materials loud and clear: "If it involves plants and is creative, I have done it or want to do it."

Her connection to nature started early in life: "I have a bit of a hippie background; part of my very early childhood was spent in a squat/commune in the North Vancouver estuary known as the Maplewood Mudflats." Even while that young, she thinks nature was being imprinted on her. "I have always tried to tread lightly on the earth in my life; making art is no different. I always have the need to question where things come from, to know the origin of my materials as much as possible." She has, it seems, always been attracted to natural materials: "It's become intrinsic for me. I've nearly always used recycled, vintage/thrifted materials to create work. I'm simply not

"I never met a technique I didn't like. That said, there have been moments when I'm creating an ink drawing of an arbutus tree, using a hand-carved arbutus twig dip pen and my own handmade arbutus bark ink, when I've thought, this is pretty rad."

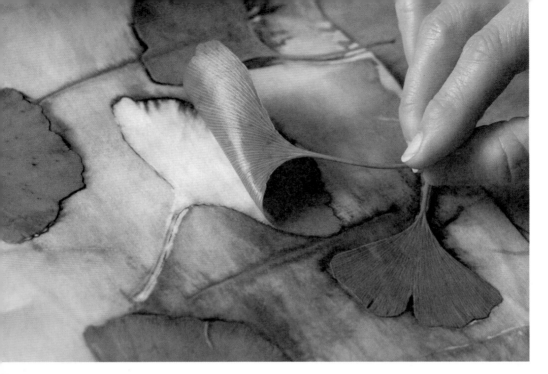

drawn to plastics or processes that are not environmentally friendly. I don't consider myself or my work important enough to make something that would not, eventually, biodegrade back into the earth."

Christi's basket-making process and techniques are closely tied to her natural materials; the final shape is often determined by what she finds. Her baskets have a look about them as if she has just picked them up, fully made, in nature. They are unassuming, natural forms: "It often starts outside, in someone's garden, down on the beach or in the woods, as I respectfully gather materials. If it's a 3D piece, I often take cues from the shape of the original vines or wood. Certain shapes will suggest the final form. These pieces will usually be an abstracted vessel form. Or I can create something flatter that can hang as a wall piece." With her works on paper, she is, she says, a bit more literal: "I find it hard to improve on Mother Nature with the shape of leaves. I definitely play with composition in my layouts for botanical printing, but I also love how the outcome is often a surprise. I'll often use flower inks/stains as spontaneous creative prompts, which leads me to create work I otherwise wouldn't have."

"I do make sure work is on archival paper, is prepared properly and will last a lifetime. But honestly, who is going to remember or care after 100 or so years? My work and life are a mere blip in the scale of civilization, never mind the history of the planet. I think it's important to remember that."

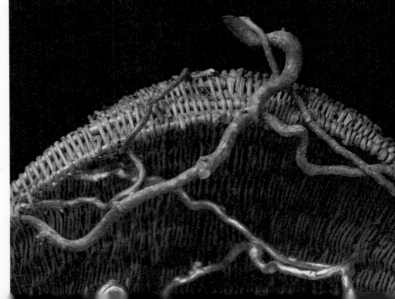

"My favourite art supply is the flotsam and jetsam of the natural world. Specifically, lately I seem to be endlessly drawn to leaves. I use all kinds of leaves both as art material and subject matter. For example, daylily leaves are a material that is used by basket makers for weaving. These are the long, thin leaves that die back at the end of the flower season and can be harvested sustainably. I use them in my 3D sculptural work quite a bit, but they are indistinguishable as leaves by the time they get woven in.

And leaves are both the subject matter and the 'art supply' in botanical contact printing. Also known as eco printing, it's a heat, dye and steam process in which the natural colours/tannins in the leaves are transferred directly onto paper or fabric. I've also started saving the flattened leaves from this process. And lately I've been combining a classic 'nature print' technique—inking the plant material and creating a print—on top of the botanical prints. I like the direction it's moving in."

Her palette of colours might also be described as found, too. And it is as harmonious as her materials (or nature) allow for: "Currently I adore muted earth tones with a pop of colour. This goes for everything from home décor to the clothing I wear. I don't think there are any colours found in nature that don't 'go together.'" And that's lucky because Christi is always looking for something new to fold into her practice: "I can't *not* make art. It's like an affliction. It's just the way my brain works. I'm very lucky to have arranged my life and made choices so I get to make art any damn day I want."

A common theme in this book is that artists who use unconventional materials as their art supplies—recycled, found and upcycled supplies in particular—feel a creative liberation through using them, as if they have been given permission to bypass the restrictive pressures that using expensive materials can bring. They feel free to experiment, to mess about, to see where the materials might take them, creatively. As Christi says: "There's something about the un-precious nature of these supplies—it's just flower petals and hot water. And it will eventually fade, so I can just relax and play." ✻

PLANT BLINDNESS

In modern life, a lot of botanical knowledge has been lost to us and the wild and wonderful intricacies, varieties and uses of plants are often overlooked. It is something Christi regrets: "I have a natural passion for plant life and I'm especially fascinated by the collective human history of using plants for everything from fibre to dye to food."

There is a phrase, "plant blindness," a tendency to ignore plant species that is especially worrying in view of the environmental mess humans have got the planet into. The phrase was thought up by botanists Elisabeth Schussler and James Wandersee in 1998, in response to a report showing that more people recognize animal species than plant ones. Plant blindness makes people less interested in plants, and plant conservation, too.

Christi hopes her art from nature might help raise awareness of this issue: "If I can open someone's eyes to the value in plant life, even a wee bit, it's very satisfying. When someone tells me that I've inspired them to try a certain technique that they've seen in my newsletter, that I've opened their eyes to the plant life around them, that's the best feeling."

WILD BASKETRY

Learning wild basketry harvesting techniques, Christi explains, goes hand in hand with learning plant identification. Her studio is piled high with bundles of daylily leaves, rolls of bark and dried vines (all responsibly foraged), prepared and ready to be used in her next creative project.

With nature as her art supply shop, she felt liberated: "When I was taught how to make cordage out of blackberry bark, it was an important moment. Learning that I could collect overlooked, undervalued plant materials and use them as 'free' art supplies set me down a creative path I've been travelling for nearly seven years."

From there, Christi remembers, it was just a hop, skip and jump to learning about making inks and dyes from plants and making tools out of found pieces. It brings that feeling of freedom to all of her practice: "Lately, I've started creating mark-making tools out of arbutus twigs and cedar bark bristles. I love the unpredictability of them. Sometimes when I hold a (normal) paintbrush, it can bring too much expectation with it."

christiyork.com
@york_christi

DA VINCI ARTIST BRUSHES

At the da Vinci brush factory in Nuremberg, Germany, they make about six million artist, craft and school brushes in a year. That is a very satisfying thought: brushes everywhere. Brushes are such lovely things. They are simple (though not to make), functional, tactile and beautiful. At da Vinci, brush makers go through a special training in which they learn the profession of "Pinselmacher," or brush maker. It takes three years. "In our sun-filled rooms masters and apprentices sit at their marble tables learning the skills of brush making," the company says. "Visitors to the facility often express surprise at the calm atmosphere not usually found in a 'factory.' They often compare it to a laboratory or studio, as the silence of concentration prevails, interrupted only by occasional consultation and conversation."

The company that became da Vinci had its beginnings in the late 19th century, when Nuremberg was home to several brush-making factories. But during the Second World War the building (and its records) were destroyed. It was then re-established by Hansfried Defet and his wife, Marianne. They chose a new brand name, "da Vinci" (first registered in 1952), to evoke the famous Renaissance artist. They hoped it would be a brand name that suited their ambition "to make the best artist brushes in the world." Today the company employs around 130 people and does indeed sell high-end artist's brushes the world over.

Hermann Meyer, co-owner of the company (with Tobias Meyer and Julian Rottner Defet), joined da Vinci out of college in 1985. He had grown up in a

"The art of brush making lies in the fact that an artist can buy a certain series and size and 10 years later can buy exactly the same quality they used before. Artists, in our experience, are very conservative and peculiar with their tools and do not like too many changes."

bookbinding and stationery family, so was somewhat familiar with the art supply landscape. Da Vinci manufactures some 12,000 different brushes. Many are the standard brushes you would hope to see: watercolour, oil and acrylic paint brushes, pastel painting brushes, impasto brushes, tempera brushes and so on. But they also make many specialist brushes, like rigger brushes (for script lettering), fan blender brushes (useful for gilding the grooves of baroque picture frames), hair mottler brushes (to grain and marble) and pinstriping brushes (for signwriting). The list can (and does) go on: "Over the years we have developed special brush shapes with many artists and have listened to their advice and requests. We have made, for example, unique brushes for artists which are half a metre wide, or have handles one metre in length—or even longer. Our aim is to supply artists with the tools they need to make their fantasies reality."

Their natural hair brushes are made by hand but most of their synthetic brushes are produced semi-automatically "on machines we construct and built in our own house and workshops." They do all the brush-making processes in-house, dressing the hair for the brushes, mixing their own synthetic fibres and so on. So they know exactly what is inside their brushes: "The better the brush—not only the hair, but also the whole balance and combination of handle, ferrule and hair/fibre—the better and more secure the artist will be at their work." ✳

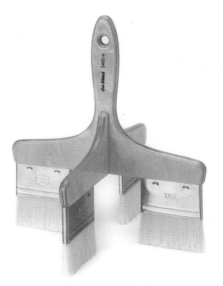

MAKING AN ARTIST'S BRUSH

When making an artist's brush, everything begins with the hairs: "By selecting only the finest quality hair, the brush can be used delicately or aggressively and give the artist optimum results." The brush maker fills a small brass case with the hair (or bristle) needed for the required brush. "The brass case is then drummed on the marble table until each hair settles to the bottom. After having retrieved the right amount of hair from the brass case, the hair will be put into a cotton spring loop that is spun between the fingers. Soon the hair is bloomed into the correct shape. The brush maker quickly fixes this shape by turning the thread again while holding the other end of the thread tightly with his teeth. At our factory the brush maker needs only a knife and a pair of scissors. The pair of scissors to cut through the string, the knife to remove from time to time hairs or bristles which are blunt or lying backwards. However, a brush maker would *never* even dream of shaping an artist brush with the knife. The handmade shape has always been and will always be the most vital quality feature of a good artist brush."

Next, the hair bundle will be placed in the metal ferrule, which must be filled snugly, and then glued using a dosing machine. "After the drying process, all the hairs are firmly positioned. Then there are other machines doing their work: handles and ferrules are pressed together, sizes and company names stamped onto the handles. Last but not least, each brush is carefully checked to see if the finishing of the brush head is impeccable and the ferrule is firmly attached to the handle."

davinci-defet.com
@davinci_artistbrushes_official

EMMA BLOCK

Emma Block is an illustrator, writer and workshop tutor with a deep love of paint. She is particularly fond of watercolours and gouache paint. So much, in fact, that she has written and illustrated books about them. Emma began working professionally as an illustrator at 17, when she started licensing her designs to greetings card companies. Ten years ago, after graduating with a bachelor's in illustration, she took the leap into full-time freelance illustrating. When not making her own work or writing books, Emma can be found sharing her processes, inspirations and materials (and various work and life meanderings) online and in her classes.

For many artists, getting to know which materials are right for you is a process of trial and error. However, one of the benefits of social media is connecting with other artists' practices and hearing about their experiences. A propinquitous Instagram post changed Emma's way of working: "Despite studying art for five years I had never even heard gouache mentioned. After I graduated from university I saw a few other illustrators using it on Instagram and decided to buy myself a set." After years painting with watercolours, discovering gouache was revelatory: "It had more substance than watercolours, it didn't have the plasticky finish of acrylics and it had a quicker drying time and easier clean-up than oil paints. It is bold yet versatile, layerable, water soluble and re-wettable, and it gives a gorgeous velvety matte finish, which makes it my perfect paint."

But she didn't leave her watercolours behind. Watercolours and gouache are now her two most

"People often say I look like my illustrations, perhaps because we share a similar colour palette, or because the people I paint often have rosy cheeks and delicate features like myself."

used mediums. Dipping between the two gives Emma options, depending on what feel she is after: "People often ask me how I choose which one I use for a project, but I just have a sort of gut feeling. They both have such unique personalities. I find watercolours to be soft, romantic, light and delicate on the page. They can feel modern and fresh, or slightly traditional." Gouache, on the other hand, plays nicely with other art supplies: "Gouache has a much bolder character; you can create such a richness of colour and texture, and it works so well with other mediums like coloured pencils. I love the versatility of gouache, the variety of textures that can be created and how you can control it with square and angled brushes. I also love the immediacy of it; gouache is quite a forgiving medium and will work well on most papers or sketchbooks, unlike watercolours which are a little bit more fussy."

In 2020 Emma turned her new love of this art supply into a book: *Get Started with Gouache*, a guide to getting started with the (often overlooked) medium of gouache. It followed her book *The Joy of Watercolour:*

40 Happy Lessons for Painting the World Around You, published in 2018, which is currently in its eighth print run. The books are full of her pretty illustrated vignettes of the everyday: everyday people doing everyday things. Emma paints and draws with a romantic palette of colours; her paintbrush touches lightly on the paper: "My work is all about colour, texture and shape, with very little line work. I think there's a softness to my work, my colours are often warm and muted and my paintings are usually vignettes with rough edges. I very rarely use the colour black. I think my work has a certain warmth to it and it makes people smile."

Emma works in a room in her Victorian flat in North London. It has big sash windows that flood the space with lots of natural light. Her mid-century-ish desk holds a mixture of digital and traditional tools. There is an iMac and a scanner and lots of interesting looking pots of brushes, pencils, pens, scissors and craft knives. She has all her art supplies to hand; it looks pretty perfect for an artist. She also has a little shelf above the desk for her sketchbooks and well-used paint palettes. "I always love how the paint palettes end up looking like a work of art themselves," she says.

The compactness and neatness of her working space makes sense when you look at her work, which is mainly on a small scale—and when you realize how efficiently she works, too: "I can often fit several spot illustrations on one sheet of A4 paper and a tube of paint can last me for many years. Where it's possible I buy materials that are made in the UK, like St Cuthberts Mill paper, made in Somerset, or Pro Arte brushes, made in Yorkshire. One of the best ways to reduce consumption is to look after what you already have. My sable watercolour brushes used to belong to my grandpa and are still in great shape." ✳

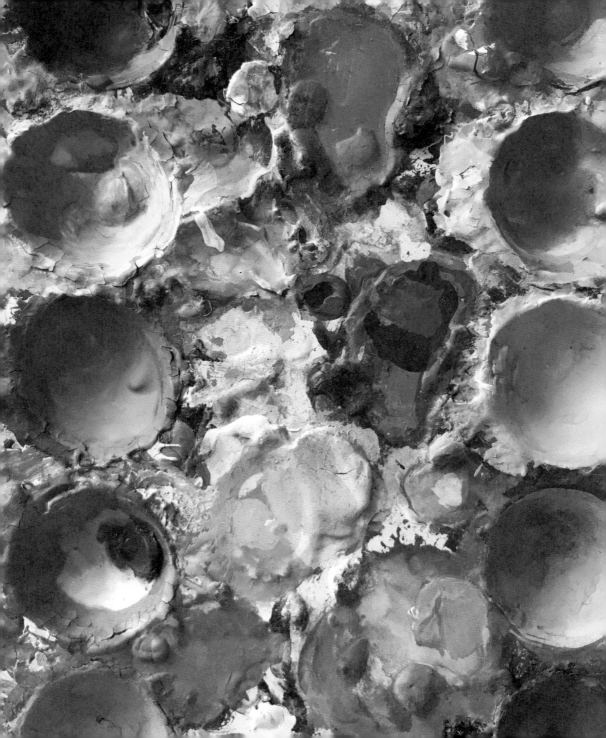

TO SKETCH
(DIGITAL OR NOT)

Emma's most used creative tool at the moment is her iPad Pro: "I use it for sketching and it's such a timesaver. Instead of sketching in pencil on loose sheets of paper, then scanning the sketches, editing them on Photoshop, merging different sketches together and sending it to the client, I can just do the whole thing in one go on my iPad and send the sketch straight to the client." She was surprised, though, to find that she enjoyed working on a screen: "The 6B brushes in Procreate are so good you would never know it's not a real pencil. I never thought I would be sketching digitally, but it just really works for me." Once she is happy with her sketch, Emma prints it out, paperclips it to a piece of watercolour or cartridge paper and puts it on her lightbox: "I've had my lightbox for over 10 years. It's almost falling apart but I love it." Working using a light box means there are no pencil lines under the artwork, which gives the final painting a fresh, crisp look. She loves to listen to podcasts when she paints: "If I'm working on a big project I might work on several paintings at once. I occasionally add finishing details with some coloured pencils, then I scan it into my computer and clean it up in Photoshop, if necessary. I don't edit my work much, it's usually just a case of cleaning up shadows at the edge of the paper and then it's ready to be sent to the client."

emmablock.co.uk
@emmablockillustration

ENCAUSTIFLEX

Artists who think creatively and often out of the box make great problem solvers. And once they have user-tested their own invention and solved a problem to their satisfaction, they sometimes find themselves running businesses selling their problem solvers to other people. Leslie Giuliani is a painter and textile artist and educator—and a solver of a very specific creative problem. "I wanted to somehow merge my encaustic painting practice with my machine embroidery work," she explains. "But I was flummoxed to find a substrate to paint with wax and then stitch into, heavily, without the paint cracking and the paper tearing due to the dense concentrations of needle perforations." And so she became the inventor of Encaustiflex. It sounds suitably scientific but is actually quite simple. Encaustiflex is a material made from spun polyester and nylon, partially sourced from recycled soda bottles.

Sourcing samples from the manufacturer (the material was used for various industrial purposes such as cleaning cloths and soundproofing), Leslie discovered a material that worked well for her purpose. "The embroideries can contain tens of thousands of stitches, which can rip paper to shreds. Encaustiflex does not rip so I could pile on the stitches even after I painted the background with encaustic paint." She wrote to the manufacturer and sent them photos of what she was doing. They were delighted and sent a whole roll of it to her, along with a book of other samples to try. She chose three weights that served different needs, out of the dozens that the company makes: "They

"Artists can use a limited number of excellent materials in myriad ways that work well with each other. You do not need every art supply! Get to know your materials and try to use things that play well together. I like to think Encaustiflex is one of those go-to materials."

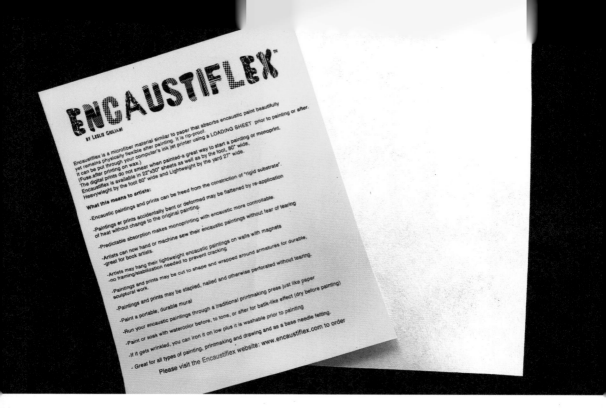

ENCAUSTIFLEX™

BY LESLIE GIULIANI

Encaustiflex is a microfiber material similar to paper that absorbs encaustic paint beautifully yet remains physically flexible after painting. It is rip-proof.

It can be put through your computer's ink jet printer using a LOADING SHEET prior to painting or after. (Fuse after printing on wax.)

The digital prints do not smear when painted—a great way to start a painting or monoprint. Encaustiflex is available in 22"x30" sheets as well as by the foot, 80" wide.

Heavywieght by the foot 60" wide and Lightweight by the yard 27" wide.

What this means to artists:

-Encaustic paintings and prints can be freed from the constriction of "rigid substrate".

-Paintings or prints accidentally bent or deformed may be flattened by re-application of heat without change to the original painting.

-Predictable absorption makes monoprinting with encaustic more controllable.

-Artists can now hand or machine sew their encaustic paintings without fear of tearing -great for book artists.

-Artists may hang their lightweight encaustic paintings on walls with magnets -no framing/stabilization needed to prevent cracking

-Paintings and prints may be cut to shape and wrapped around armatures for durable, sculptural work.

-Paintings and prints may be stapled, nailed and otherwise perforated without tearing.

-Paint a portable, durable mural

-Run your encaustic paintings through a traditional printmaking press just like paper

-Paint or soak with watercolor before, to tone, or after for batik-like effect (dry before painting)

- If it gets wrinkled, you can iron it on low plus it is washable prior to painting

- Great for all types of painting, printmaking and drawing and as a base needle felting.

Please visit the Encaustiflex website: www.encaustiflex.com to order

suggested I personally brand and market them as art supplies." She did just that, billing it as "a microfiber material similar to paper that absorbs encaustic paint beautifully, yet remains physically flexible after painting."

Leslie has a bachelor of fine arts in drawing and painting but has done textile handcrafts her whole life. From her painting studio at her house in Weston, Connecticut, she works, teaches and puts Encaustiflex through its paces. Her own work uses digital embroidery, collage and a computerized sewing machine to stitch drawings onto painted, drawn or printed background paintings with Encaustiflex as the substrate. Leslie's use of encaustic as her primary paint demonstrates that she is drawn to the excitement of a messy art supply material. Encaustics are a pigmented beeswax-based paint that requires heating to become liquid and paintable. Heated palettes and tools are part of a basic encaustic setup and Leslie also pulls a few other favourites into her daily art practice:

"I use other paints and inks that are compatible with encaustic as well. Brushes, mark-making tools, wooden substrates are all handy for me and my students' needs. As a core support instructor, I also work with R&F Handmade Paints (R&F manufactures the encaustic, oil-based pigment sticks that I use in my artwork), so I have tons of beautiful paint."

Leslie uses machine embroidery software that is traditionally used to design and stitch logos onto hats and tote bags. Ten years ago, she began to focus on digital embroidery after seeing examples of it used as part of a fine arts practice at Judith Solodkin's New York printmaking studio. Judith was Louise Bourgeois's master printer and Louise was known for her embroidered books. "Judith editioned them for MOMA and other collectors. I knew I had to learn how," says Leslie. She interned with a commercial embroiderer for over a year, doing logos for garments and tote bags to learn the technical aspects of designing, programming and stitching out. Whilst she loved finally creating embroideries of her own, she wanted to meld her encaustic painting practice with her embroideries: "I needed to find a material that could handle both together. I found that encaustic worked beautifully on Encaustiflex. I could paint and print on it, layer after layer, and then embroider *through* the paint."

It was only after this material solved her own problem that Leslie sent it out into the world. Named to describe its unique attributes, Encaustiflex encourages other artists to work free of traditionally rigid substrates to create art that is flexible in physical form—art that is completely up to the imagination and ingenuity of the maker. ✳

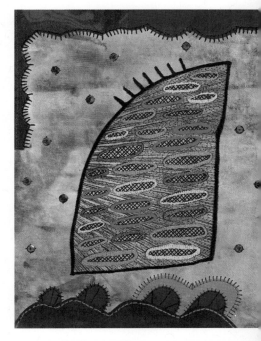

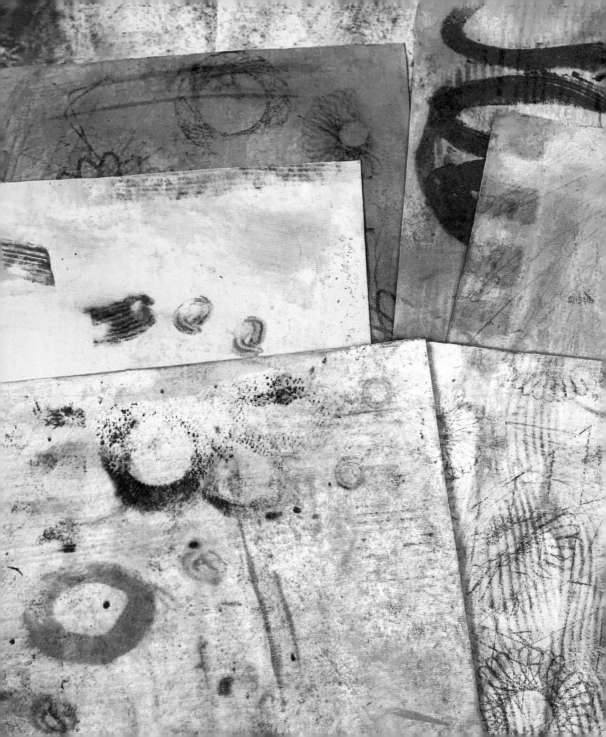

THE MANY USES OF ENCAUSTIFLEX

Rather like Leslie, Encaustiflex is a problem solver: "It works well with so many other art materials that artists are sure to find a fit for it in their art-making practice. Textile artists can weave and sew it. Painters of all media can paint on it. Printmakers love its stability and toughness. Artists have even cut it to string beads. It can be used sculpturally because it can be hammered, stapled and grommeted without ripping—almost endless possibilities."

Leslie likes the fact that, in her own work, she can keep building interesting layers onto it: "Encaustiflex is spectacularly absorbent. It can hold layers and layers of paint so I can create a richly nuanced surface to embroider on. Sometimes I like to begin my layering process with suminagashi marbling. Encaustiflex grabs onto the ink pattern without smearing. Encaustiflex does not deform when wet. I can dry it and overprint layers of suminagashi. The results are wild!"

Painted and printed Encaustiflex can also be cut and woven without fraying. It likes acrylic and it is great for traditional printmaking with a press because it does not stretch or shred, wet or dry. Leslie even runs it through her inkjet printer—probably not something included in the manufacturer's handbook.

encaustiflex.com
@encaustiflex

FERRIS WHEEL PRESS

Ferris Wheel Press was established in 2010 in Markham, Ontario. They began as a custom correspondence and event stationery design firm, specializing in creating hand-illustrated designs for clients and bringing them to life with in-house letterpress printing, on machines dating back to 1904. After years of telling clients' stories, they decided it was time to tell their own, and Ferris Wheel Press was born. The first products they made were fountain pens, fountain pen ink and fine paper goods. Their Brush fountain pen, a signature product, arrived in 2016, followed by their first collection of fountain pen inks in 2018 in the colours Candy Marsala, Tanzanite Sky and their now signature ink Bluegrass Velvet.

The company is named for the Ferris wheel that resides at the Canadian National Exhibition, an annual festival held in Toronto in the days leading up to Canadian Labour Day (the first Monday in September). There has been a Ferris wheel at the Exhibition since it opened in 1912. "Our co-founders [Raymond Yu and Deborah Lau-Yu] shared a romantic Ferris wheel ride at the Exhibition on their first date over a decade ago," explains vice president Jimmy Yu. Taking on both the historical lore and longevity of the Ferris wheel, the carnival attraction as company iconography also acts as a metaphor. "That experience became a defining moment for us, as the view is always the best at the top of the Ferris wheel."

Ferris Wheel Press is known for its fine stationery; ink is packaged in baroque bottles, with romantic names, and sold in (arguably) even more covetable,

"At Ferris Wheel Press, everything begins with the ideation of a story that is inspired by our history in printing, and our mission to help the world fall in love with writing again. Every ink collection is created to tell a story, and immerse our fans in a world of imagination."

ornate packaging. Jimmy, who oversees art direction, product design, marketing and branding, is a graphic designer by training. He developed the distinctive curvaceous graphic look and feel that pays homage to letterpress printing machines and the hand-painted sign writing and swirls on traditional fairground merry-go-rounds and Ferris wheels. The products and packaging designs are developed through many iterations. Ink is often inspired by a specific colour and the feeling it evokes is evident in the packaging. At other times, they take a special moment or a memory and work backwards to define a colour that best represents it: "There is no hard and fast rule and any time you try to put a creative endeavour on a straight line, you are already limiting its full potential."

Ferris Wheel Press offers a palette of over 40 fountain pen ink colours, with hues ranging from sheening inks to sparkling inks, bright to muted colours, annual limited-edition colours and collaborations with local and international brands. Ink is made by hand using a combination of natural and synthetic dyes added to distilled water: "Our inks are rigorously tested for stability and tone. For any given tone, there could be six to eight variants that are created, compared and tested against. We look at colour tone, shading and consistency, sheens, sparkle shades, swatching and writing performance, among other things." As head creative and designer, it is hard for Jimmy to select just one favourite colour. But he does explain why he particularly likes a sparkly jade ink: "One of our latest inks is Moonlit Jade, a special-edition ink collaboration, conceptualized with a local cultural platform called Fête Chinoise. It was created to celebrate Lunar New Year and the year of the tiger. I love it because of the rich jade-inspired tone and the glistening silver sparkle that makes it a beautiful highlight. It can spruce up any piece of writing, even something as mundane as a daily priorities list." Jimmy is specific about his

HEADQUARTERS

"Creating inks is a colourful, messy and beautiful adventure. Ferris Wheel Press' studio houses 25-plus full-time members, consisting of our dedicated team of illustrators and designers, sales and marketing team with in-house photography capabilities, production, quality control and fulfillment teams. In addition to these spaces, we also house a collection of vintage letterpress printing machines—some that date back to 1912—and type cabinets, as well as a showroom and library of our archived projects."

fountain pen preference though: "After writing with a fountain pen for several years now, I prefer medium to broader nibs, as the increased ink flow really showcases the characteristics that we work so hard to create in our inks, beautifully demonstrating the sheen, shading and sparkles."

Hues such as Bluegrass Velvet, Stroke of Midnight, Tokyo Bay Blue and Wonderland in Coral set one's imagination (and writing) on fire. "Our inspiration is drawn from Canadian themes; we look at the iconic, as well as humble landscapes and historical architecture that define our beautiful country. And the beautiful animals too. We also explore local communities and ideas that are a part of our teams' childhoods. And we also look at the memories and inspirations from our travels." Of course, an ink fountain pen is not just for writing a daily priorities list or journal entry, and they have seen their inks used to make line drawings, watercolours, lettering and calligraphy. Pen-and-ink are for anything you might wish to put down on paper. And Ferris Wheel Press has just the right shade to help you do it. ✳

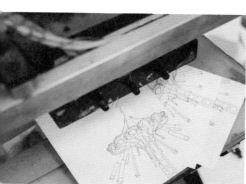

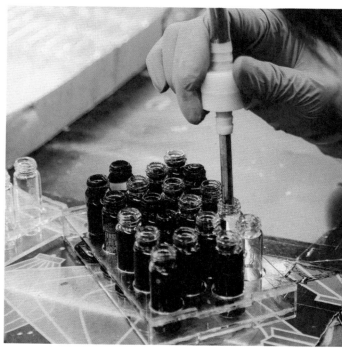

Fall in Love with Writing again

ROARING PATINA BLACK
PATINE NOIRE

ROARING PATINA BLACK
COLOUR PROFILE

FINE NIB BRUSH FOUNTAIN PEN	
MEDIUM NIB BRUSH FOUNTAIN PEN	
GLASS DIP PEN	
SWATCH	
SWATCH	

3x   2x   1x

ferriswheelpress.com
@ferriswheelpress

WHY WRITE?

At Ferris Wheel Press they take writing seriously—not just because they make pens and ink but because of the power of the *act* of writing. Jimmy explains: "Writing has changed my life, and many others' at Ferris Wheel Press, in some form. You don't need to be writing novels for it to be transformative. Building a habit of writing daily goals has helped to shape my thinking and my routine." Lots of people have found that the slow act of writing—with a pen, on crisp paper, in a lovely journal—can help them with arranging their thoughts and with their mental health too. "It has also made noticeable improvements in my short- and long-term memory," says Jimmy. "Free-flowing writing can be quite telling for spotting where you are emotionally and spiritually. And continued writing naturally helps you organize your thoughts and gain clarity." Putting his own pen to paper, then, has been a side benefit of running Ferris Wheel Press: "This has been huge for me, as Ferris Wheel Press continues to grow and decisions become more weighted."

GRACE HORNE

G race Horne works out of "Steel City," Sheffield, England, making knives and one-off artisan scissors. Her workshop—a converted public toilet workshop—has "typical Victorian architectural attention to detail with dressed stone walls and original glazed bricks. It is tiny, quirky and perfect for me," she says. Her metalwork is both contemporary and also deeply embedded within historical Sheffield knife making: "I made my first knives in 1991 as a final year degree project. My parents always carried basic working folding knives, and making pocket knives seemed the ideal project. I had tried to contact Sheffield knife makers but the lack of response lead me to believe that there were none still working, so I just figured it out as I went along."

Grace later heard an interview on the radio with Stan Shaw, a local "little mester" (or small-scale master craftsman). "I decided to come to Sheffield to see what I could learn," she says. "Unfortunately, he was unable to take on an apprentice, so I decided to take a more academic approach, completing both a knife-related master's degree and a PhD at Sheffield Hallam University. Finally, after nearly 15 years in Sheffield, I got to do a research project that allowed me to work with the knife makers who I had originally come to Sheffield to work with." Grace became a little mester, of sorts, herself—historically they were self-employed men who rented workspace in the cutlery factories. "I have always had a desire to learn new skills, and around seven years ago I persuaded Ernest Wright & Son, one of the last scissor makers in Sheffield, to

"Good tools can make creating objects a joy; and good tools made with love and care can be repaired and re-sharpened and passed down to future generations."

teach me to make scissors. I only intended to make scissors as an element in my folding knives but they currently seem to have a life all of their own."

Grace works alone in her converted studio: "There is just me. Sometimes I collaborate with other craftspeople but generally it's just me—from the initial design, cutting it out of sheet steel, shaping it with files, to packaging and dispatching." She mainly uses steel in her scissors, although she sometimes mixes it with other materials. Grace uses one of three different methods for getting the basic shape in steel to make each pair of her scissors, known as "preparing the blank." The method she uses depends on the design and what she wants to achieve. The first method is the most traditional: "I collaborate with a blacksmith to get forms rough-forged to my design. I usually make a full-size wooden model of my designs, so we work to that as well as my drawings. Hand forging scissors is a skilled and specialist task and rarely attempted today. These rough forgings need to be prepared for the next stage by establishing flat surfaces and by refining the overall shapes by hand filing."

The second method is "stock removal," in which two identical halves are cut out of sheet steel, usually by hacksaw—or a fine jeweller's saw, if the detail is fine and the scissors are delicate. This method is the simplest but the most wasteful of material. The third method is the most radical but it allows her to "pattern match" her steel as if it were dressmaking fabric: "Using wire electrical discharge machining, I cut the entire profile as a though it were a pair of closed scissors and then cut down the middle of the blade to create two cutting surfaces. It is an incredibly accurate but slow process. However, when I use it on a piece of patterned steel, it ensures that the pattern in the steel matches across the entire pair of scissors when it is reassembled. To my knowledge, I am the only person who has ever made scissors this way."

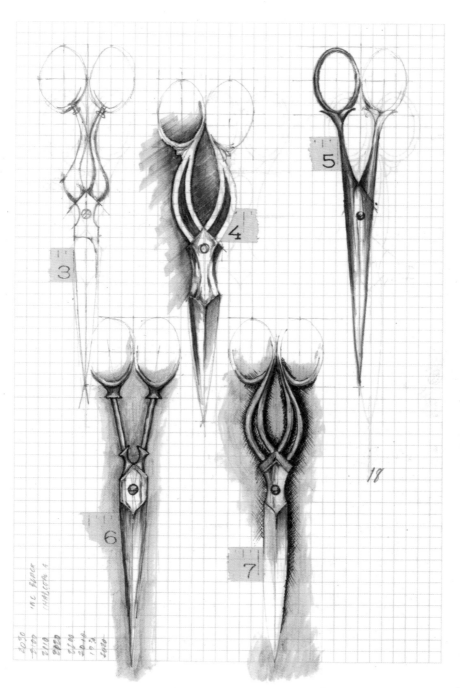

3

4

5

6

7

18

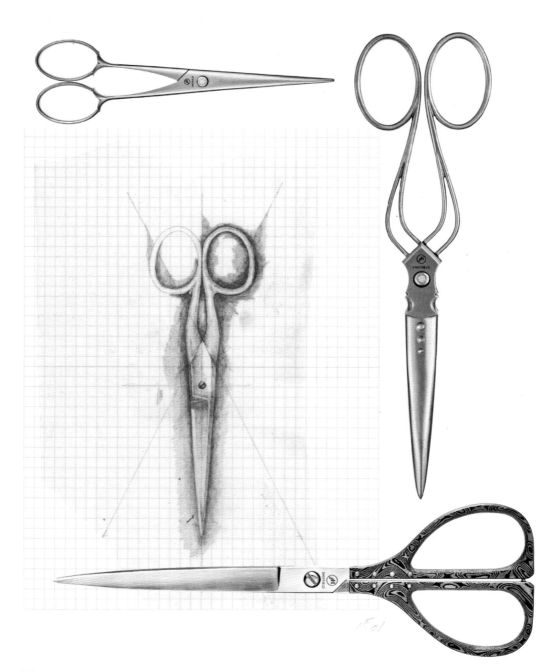

Grace will then "establish the cutting mechanism" of her scissors: "Although it seems counterintuitive, the first area to refine is where the two finger bows touch." Whichever way her scissor blanks have been made, the next step is to grind the internal cutting surfaces at a subtle angle, to ensure that the blades only touch along their cutting edge when they are in use: "At this point, I also stamp on the pair marks. These are done just behind the pivot surface and are only visible when the scissors are open wide. This was traditionally done to ensure that, in a batch, the two halves were always paired up correctly when they were finally assembled."

To get the pivot point of the scissors—where they are joined—one half is drilled with a clearance hole and counterbored on the outside, so that the head of the screw can sit just below the surface. The bottom half is drilled and the thread is tapped. At this point, the scissors can be joined with a temporary screw and all the subtle shaping of the form takes place. The finger bows (holes) are shaped to make them comfortable, and the delicacy of the shanks is filed in. The external shaping to get the gentle curve of the blades is now done. The two halves of the scissors are then heat treated, bound together with iron wire to maintain the blade curve, then hardened and tempered in their bound state. They are only hardened up to the end of the blade—the bows and shanks are kept softer for any final adjustments. Then it is a matter of cleaning the hardened pieces. The cutting surfaces get stoned and polished, and, if the scissors are made from patterned

"Many craft practitioners are pleasure driven: making brings them joy. Using tools that have been crafted with love increases the pleasure and the feeling of connectedness with other creatives."

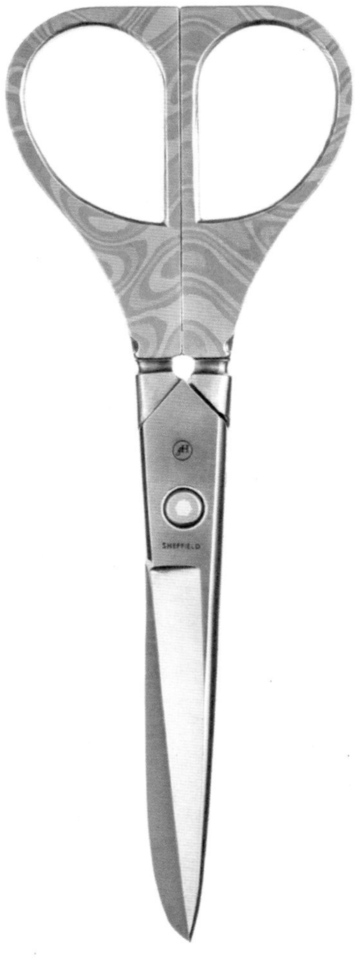

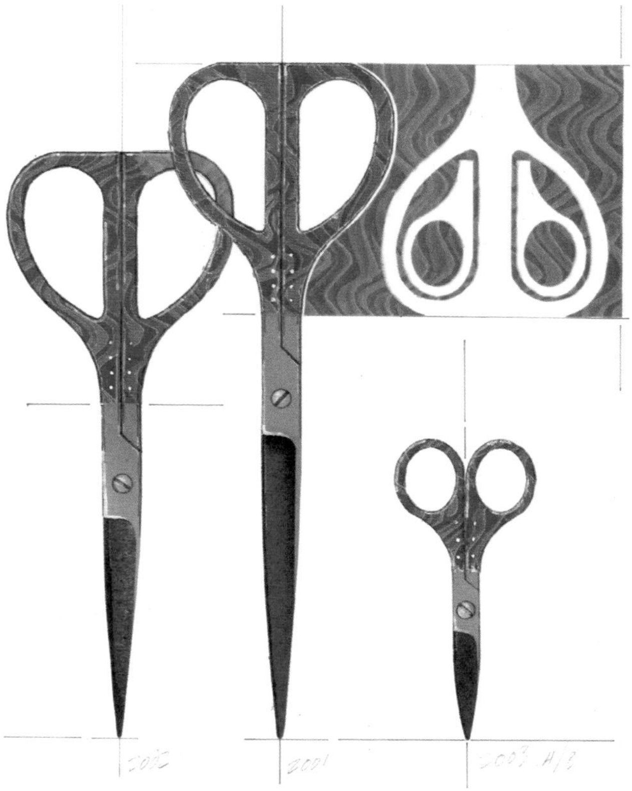

steel, the surface is etched to reveal the pattern. The final stage involves setting a new screw, doing a final test and then the riveting over of the screw end to stop it undoing during use.

Grace loves to share her knowledge and experience, as well as her passion, for scissor making. She does live sessions on social media, talking about how scissors are made and showing historical examples. She also does online "critical clinic" mentoring, in which people send her scissors they have made and she gives them feedback on correction and improvements. It is lovely to think of her working from the city that once employed men and women who had just the same skillset she has—to know that her scissors are cut in the same place as so many other pairs were. But her work is also imbued with her own personality and artisanal touch, giving us some of the loveliest scissors you could hope to use. ✻

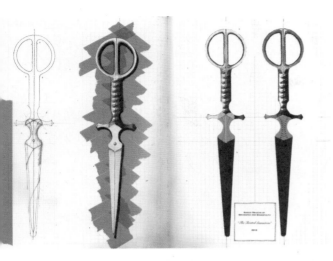

CELEBRATING THE CREATIVE PROCESS

Years of working within a university has left me with a deep urge to research and document my process, even in my studio practice where no one will see it. I like to know the history behind the materials and processes that I use today and very often these investigations will be the start of an entire body of work. One of my surprise discoveries was the vast yet invisible female workforce within Sheffield knife making, often performed within a domestic setting. I am proud to count myself a continuation of that story, while also bringing more visibility to it.

My sketchbooks are an incredibly important part of my creative process. By the time I get to the workshop my designs are clearly laid out with details and a plan of work. I'll often make a full-size working wooden model to test the final design. I use pictures of my sketches and models on social media to start engaging my followers during the making process. I made a very complex pair of cigar scissors in gold and Damascus steel and made a plain steel prototype first. A collector of my work asked if would be prepared to sell the wooden model. I ended up making a pack for him that included a bound book of prints of my sketches and photos of my process, the little working wooden model and the plain steel prototype. He loved having the story of the creative process more than anything. The final piece was sold to another collector.

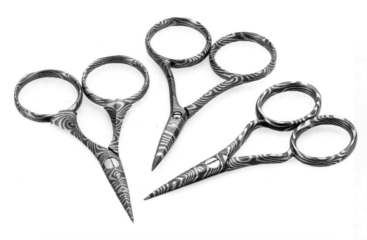

Sheffield, in South York-
shire, England, was known
as Steel City—famous for
steel and cutlery produc-
tion during the Industrial
Revolution of the 19th
century. But mentions of
knife making in the city
appear as far back as in
Geoffrey Chaucer's *Can-
terbury Tales*, written at the
end of the 14th century. The
city has a long tradition of
making exhibition pieces
within the cutlery trade.
"They were the showcase
pieces that were used to
sell the everyday smaller
pieces and were designed
to demonstrate the skill of
the company's craftsmen,"
says Grace. Her exquisite
scissors demonstrate both
her skills as a craftsman
and her love of the tool
itself: "The term 'exhibition
piece' appeals to me; it
implies a joyful exuberance
of technical skill—time
taken out of everyday work
to produce a piece that
often resulted in some-
thing so highly decorative
that it was impractical for
everyday use. Despite this
flamboyance, the pieces
still had to be functional—
blades had to be heat
treated, scissors had to cut
beautifully, silver platters
had to stand."

GREENLEAF & BLUEBERRY

Jess Greenleaf is an artist, entrepreneur, pigment hunter, cowboy camping enthusiast, colour science aficionado and rogue scholar. She has channelled a little of all of these qualities into her business, Greenleaf & Blueberry, making handmade and carefully curated art supplies for the creative traveller. Like many small business owners, Jess started out making the products she was looking for herself: "From a very young age, I was unequivocal about my intent to be an artist, but I didn't fall down the watercolour rabbit hole until I found mountaineering. As I moved through the mountains, I thought a lot about what art supplies I could carry without compromising the quality of my work or the success and safety of my climb. Watercolour was my answer. They are portable while forcing no compromise in quality and still allowing a full range of colours."

She had the drive and energy to follow her idea. She wanted to carry a paint palette that contained colours she had made herself, inspired by and sourced from the landscape. Things went better than expected and she quickly found herself making more paint than she could ever use and that other artists were interested in the idea of natural pigments: "I've always been uncomfortable with the relationship between being a maker and consumerism. Being drawn to do business by creating the colours and supplies that I wanted to use but couldn't find on the market felt natural and right." So, Greenleaf & Blueberry was born. Jess continues to work on products that are most close to her heart: "I design and sell the supplies I most want to use. Every single item that I make, design or source,

"In providing artists with a wider, more unusual spectrum of colours, we expand the potential of what they can create. Imagine what a composer might feel on discovering new musical notes?"

has to be top quality, be beautifully executed and light me up creatively. If I wouldn't personally use it, then I won't make it or sell it."

The team at Greenleaf & Blueberry in Western Colorado works intensively to produce the small but beautifully formed product line: "Our handmade watercolours are made in small and micro-batches with muller and slab, the same way they were made 200 years ago. Each colour is single pigment, artist grade and named for the pigment it contains. We offer Lapis Lazuli, Smalt, Vivianite, Celadonite, Moroccan Red Ochre, South African Chromite, Norwegian Magnetite, Limonite from Cypress and so many more." The watercolour names and packaging blend together beautifully, making one want to paint and travel in equal measure. Each palette contains a selection of earthy colours and a swatch card, and they are listed for sale "as they cure," fresh from their production.

Greenleaf & Blueberry also has a bindery, where they create hand-bound watercolour sketchbooks using Arches watercolour paper. And then there are the limited collections of hand-carved swizzle stick paintbrushes, featuring an intricate handle design that Jess carves: "I think of them as utilitarian sculptures, art for the artist." They also have a woodshop for making wooden travel boxes, for keeping these special paintbrushes safe. As Jess explains, as a small team of six specialists (including herself and her partner) they are in a great position to follow their own product whims: "We are purposefully and joyously small, which allows us to create our more fantastic and impractical items, such as single-pigment genuine natural top-grade Lapis Lazuli, Meteorite made from (you guessed it) real meteorites, and watercolours housed in natural seashells as a plastic-free alternative to typical watercolour pans. All of these items are expensive, rare and labour intensive. Larger companies have to worry about competitive price points,

Greenleaf &
Blueberry

HANDMADE
WATERCOLORS

Greenleaf &
Blueberry

HANDMADE
WATERCOLORS

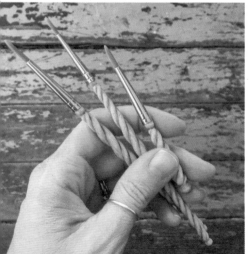

shelf life and display footprints. Being small means we can offer unicorn products without compromise or limitations."

Making the products she wants to use herself means there is a passion and commitment to the business that appeals to the end customer—likely someone committed to buying less, but better: Jess works on the premise that art supplies that are inspiring to use will be used more often: "I love the idea of blending art and utility, which is precisely how I ended up being an artist who creates art supplies. Our products are extremely labour intensive and unapologetically niche. We fuse fantasy, history, artistry and science into art supplies that could have existed a hundred years ago. I am an art supply nerd and collector, through and through, and I am the customer that I always satisfy first." ✻

ANSWERING A NEED

"Ethics, environmental impact and utility are the crossroads where every product we make begins its journey," says Jess. "We prefer for our products to answer a need and fill gaps in the market, which is very much how we ended up in business in the first place: by offering colours made with pigments that weren't being used anywhere else. Being a maker forces a reckoning with both capitalism and consumerism. If I'm not making something unique or offering a version of a product at a demonstrably higher quality, I'm really not interested in spending time on it."

The company is proud to provide quality jobs in their own town, and the ability to oversee the entire production process is important. "By using natural materials, our business is putting more dollars into renewable resources. And by creating and offering products that are high in quality, they will last longer and require fewer replacements. We are also committed to plastic-free packaging and shipping materials, and using recycled and natural materials wherever possible."

USER TESTED

All of Greenleaf & Blueberry's different products, from handmade watercolours to downloadable paintable projects, to hand-bound sketchbooks and wooden brush boxes, begin at the same place: as a prototype or test batch, user-tested by Jess: "I research, design and use myself for months or even years. Once a new product has been green-lit for production, we do loads more research on raw materials to nail down quality and responsible sources. Pigments for our handmade watercolours are researched, sourced and then put through a series of test batches."

After passing the initial set of tests, the watercolours then undergo recipe creation, and perfecting a new colour recipe can take over a year. When it finally comes time to sit down and make a colour, pigment and binder are measured and weighed precisely according to the recipe using laboratory scales. Pigment and binder are then combined and mulled together by hand using a muller and slab. Natural pigments from the same mine or location can vary, so minor adjustments are then made, depending on a variety of factors. Once a colour has been thoroughly mulled, it is put into plastic or metal pans, or natural seashells, to then sit and cure before being wrapped by hand and shipped off to customers.

Wonderland Set

Pipestone	Potter's Pink	Quinacridone Magenta	Moroccan Red Ochre	Red Earth	Pyrrole Red	Orange Ochre	Yellow Ochre	Limonite	Quinox. Yellow	Green Earth	Green Earth 2
Celadonite	Green Opalite	Potter's Green	Phthalo. Green	Vivianite	Chilean Lapis Lazuli	Smalt	Verditer	Ultramarine Blue	Phthalo. Cyan	Indanthrone Blue	French Violet Earth
Violet Hematite	Ultramarine Purple	Dioxazine Violet	Brown Ochre	Cassel Earth	Chromite	Slate	Graphite	Grey Ochre	Magnetite	Vine Charcoal	Eggshell

Greenleaf & Blueberry
HANDMADE WATERCOLORS
Professional Grade · Single-Pigment Colors · Handmade With Muller & Made in Colorado

"It should be a given that quality art supplies
offer you confidence, but they should also make
you feel wild to create with them."

Greenleaf & Blueberry use pigments from all over the world: "from gum arabic from Africa to wood from family land in the heart of the Missouri Ozark foothills," describes Jess. "Our pigments are all professional grade from established mines and sources, from as nearby as Colorado and as far away as Iceland and Australia. Gum arabic is available in a variety of different qualities and we only use the highest-tier grade and process it ourselves from the raw form to incorporate into our proprietary watercolour binder."

The wood they use is from fallen trees. "When my parents notice a down walnut tree, they haul it undercover and let us know. My partner, Matt, and my father mill the wood and stack it to begin drying. After drying in Missouri for about a year, we bring them here to continue curing in our dry Western Colorado air. Walnut that has been air dried (instead of kiln dried) is much darker, and quite rare. My mother plants walnut saplings from the Missouri Department of Conservation's State Forest Nursery to replace the fallen trees. Because we begin with raw materials and do so much processing in-house, our products have a feel and personality all their own."

JEANNE OLIVER

Giving oneself permission to make art can sometimes come with a little dose of guilt, particularly when balanced against the traditional role of parenting, or the so-called more important things that demand our attention. Some of us put our creative callings aside altogether, dedicating years to bringing up children or to working in professions far removed from creativity. There can be a sense of time running fast (or even running out) and it can be difficult to reclaim our creative selves.

It is not happenstance that artist-entrepreneur Jeanne Oliver's community is designed to get people back onto a creative path. It was her journey, too.

Growing up, Jeanne dreamed of going to art school and becoming a fashion designer but was talked out of it. Lacking the self-confidence to go against those around her, she majored in psychology and history instead. After many years when she felt she had lost her way, she became a mom and her creativity started once again to burn: "It started simply with scrapbooking, then altered journals, sketching and then painting. It grew with practice and honouring that an artist is what I had always been."

Now, from her purpose-built studio in the town of Castle Rock, Colorado, Jeanne is an author, teacher and coach through an online art school. "We have over 60,000 members and our courses include art, lifestyle and even business courses," describes Jeanne. "Creativity is calling" is the motto that greets visitors to Jeanne's virtual school. There is a class for almost everything, taught by Jeanne and a plethora of other

"I know the power of connecting with my creativity physically, emotionally and spiritually. If I do not honour it with my time and energy, no one else will fight for it for me."

artists and educators. "This gathering place is for art and lifestyle workshops no matter your experience level," Jeanne tells visitors. "Let's give ourselves the permission to be amateurs and the gift of practice. Being a creative person and living a creative life has far less to do with perfect art and more with being present and showing up. Let's start where we are, with what we have and become the artists we have dreamed to be."

"I feel like the luckiest person in the world that my life and career get to be dipped in beauty," she reflects. There are difficult days, certainly, and running a business is challenging. "But because I followed my creativity I live in a world of books, art supplies, connecting with nature, travel, teaching, learning, making, gathering... I can not even imagine a more beautiful life. All of the things that are my gifts and passions get to be rolled up to allow me to live out a life of purpose and calling. Art has allowed to me rise to a better version of myself again and again. I know the power of creating in my own life and I am so passionate because I get to share this with others and then watch them take steps to honour their own creativity."

"My art is for anyone who connects with even one element of the story and it is also for those who don't. Just because a person doesn't take it home doesn't mean that they do not have a new appreciation of the process and the artist—when we take the time to share the journey, they can."

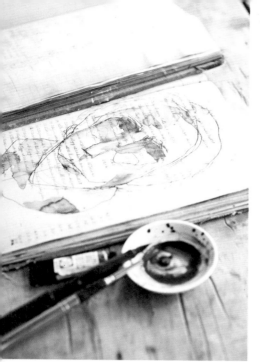

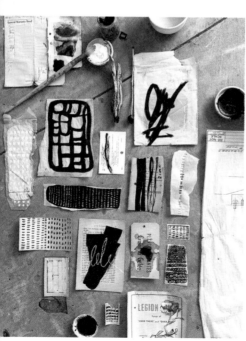

In her own art Jeanne likes to work with materials that have some patina of history to them: "As a child, I wanted to be an artist, writer, singer or actress but also an archeologist. Go figure! I believe it is that archeologist in me that is drawn to vintage ephemera. Vintage elements have always been a part of my work, even from the beginning. The fonts, textures and history has given my work layers and story separate from me. I love elements and supplies that bring grittiness and rawness to my work. I gravitate towards layers, inks, papers, plaster, charcoal, natural pigments, thick oils and cold wax. I am drawn to cardboard boxes, old pieces of wood, worn fabrics, vintage ephemera and elements from nature. I hope that by seeing the beauty in the tossed away I am able to bring items back to life. Their story then becomes a layer in my own."

There might be a metaphor at work here. As a late (art) starter, when Jeanne speaks about layers and peeling back surfaces, perhaps she is referencing how she uncovered her own confidence—how she dug deep to make her own story one with art at its centre.

"My favourite creative tool is anything that leaves a mark in a wet medium, whether it is a skewer, knife, pottery tool or even a mechanical pencil. What can I grab that will not only make a mark in a wet medium but reveal the layer underneath? The underneath is often exactly what needed to be brought forth."

"Through mark making, layers and mixed media, I hope to convey that we all have a story to tell and that second chances are waiting for each of us." Jeanne has created a space where education and inspiration are illuminated by personal experience. It is a place of journeying, sharing and making—for the possibility that dwells within all of us. ✳

"My style is definitely in the unpolished and imperfect. I gravitate towards vintage patinas, old papers, bits of plaster, old negatives, layers, torn elements and stitched fabrics."

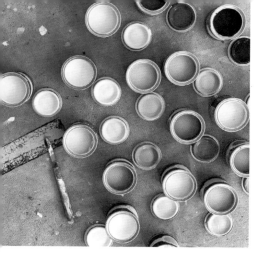

SHOWING UP

"Just being in my creative space inspires me as I organize my supplies or vintage ephemera, or even look at previous work." For Jeanne the simple act of "showing up" gets her heart and head dreaming up new ideas, projects or marks.

There are days when that might just mean a single mark on paper, because of other responsibilities. And then there are the days when she can focus longer: "Over the years I have learned that the process is more about showing up than anything else. Some days the process is studying previous work to draw out a mark that I want to use again, other days it is editing down my supplies so I will make faster decisions creatively once I begin, other days I have no idea what my first mark will be but I put something down and that one mark leads to the other, which leads to the other."

Jeanne is motivated by her own need to make and do but is also called to share what she learns with others. "To authentically make art is to make it first for me. To trust my instincts and allow myself to play and experiment. I love when a piece turns out, but I have learned more through the pieces that don't."

Hers is a journey many can relate to. Perhaps that is what makes her such a successful teacher. When she teaches a course, it is always based upon something she feels able to share with the community through her own creative journey: "That wonder to keep learning helps me as an artist, and then that is part of what makes me passionate to share it with others."

STUDIO

Jeanne's light-filled studio is the gorgeous setting of her course videos and a wonderful venue for in-person workshops when circumstances allow. Being surrounded by a wooded property naturally encourages exploration. "Nature is crucial to my own creativity and inspiration," says Jeanne. "Each day I take walks without my phone or distraction, spend time weeding the garden or even take a break from work to put my feet to the ground while I sip a cup of tea. Nature helps me to disconnect from a loud world, and in turn helps me to connect to my creativity."

While Jeanne is grateful for this abundance, she is adept at transforming any space into a creative one—and encourages her students to think this way, too. "When I first started creating again it was at the kitchen table, later our unfinished basement, then we converted our unused dining room into my studio space. Six years ago we bought a home and land with a workshop on the property that we converted to be not only my studio but a place to gather other creatives. This new space with its paint-splattered concrete floors, views of nature all around and floor-to-ceiling glass and metal garage doors is my favourite place on earth. But at the time, I would have said that about the kitchen table, unfinished basement and dining room. Creating transforms any space." Indeed, because the greatest transformation happens within us.

JENNIFER ORKIN LEWIS

Jennifer Orkin Lewis paints most days, inspired by her inner muse but prompted by an inner drive. In 2010 she left behind 20 years as a professional textile designer for a less predictable life as an illustrator. By 2014 she had started making daily 30-minute sketchbook paintings and posting them on Instagram. Her new career unfolded from there. Jennifer continues to post on social media every day, not hiding the messes or mistakes: "I try to be as straightforward and honest as I can. My pictures aren't always perfect; I may have had a tough day painting. I try to put it all out there to share the struggle."

From her base in New York in a converted garage studio—a space full of light and possibilities—Jennifer paints and illustrates, runs classes and writes books. Her subjects include charming vignettes of life, flowers, animals and people (often women) she finds inspiring. Her palette is colourful and joyous. And her use of space on the page or canvas is (not surprisingly) quite inspired by textiles: more often than not her illustrations will spread to fill all the space available to them. "My work is intuitive, colourful, textural and very often influenced by nature," she says. "My daily interactions have a huge impact on what I am possessed to paint each day. I tend to be a bit impulsive and don't have the patience for small details and laborious processes. My painting reflects that spontaneous side of me. I want to get it out and onto the surface as quickly as possible. I can slow down and be more deliberate, and I often do, but my happiest moments of painting are when I let loose."

"I love a paintbrush. Sometimes if I need to write something I prefer to write with a paintbrush rather than with a pen. There is something so comforting about a brush, the feeling of paint flowing onto the paper and seeing colour spreading out."

This relaxed work style was a much-needed antidote. "While I was in the textile industry, I was more of an art director and manager, and over time it became sort of soul crushing for me." Painting is now an integral part of her life, if not the backbone of it. If she goes a few days without it, she finds herself with too much pent-up energy and needs to pick up her brush again. "It wasn't always this way. I didn't make any artwork for 20 years while I was a stylist in the textile industry. I looked at, purchased and art-directed many things but I didn't make my own. I lost my centre at that time. When I finally got back it still took me a long time to get to where I am now. I dabbled in many different mediums and styles. When I finally started my daily sketchbook in 2014, that was when I found my path."

When Jennifer left to go on her own as an illustrator, her art supply of choice was paint, specifically acrylic gouache. It was the first paint she had used in her textile years and is the one she still reaches for first. But she also likes to add in other mediums, from oil pastels, ink and Derwent Inktense blocks (sticks of watercolour ink) to coloured pencils. "Gouache has the ability to be layered light on dark and dark on light, so I can really play with values and depth. I also love using ink and a nib pen because of the randomness I can create with lines and the occasional blob. The pencils and crayons give an interesting new texture and depth to the work."

Breaking in new art supplies requires a commitment of time and experimentation: "Each time I switch to a new type of paint it takes many many paintings to get to a point where I am comfortable with the texture and quality. I generally can get there but it takes a lot of work." Her paintings are usually made on paper, in a sketchbook and also on individual sheets of paper, but she has recently worked on wood panels and canvas, too.

Through experience and dedicated practice, Jennifer knows what will motivate her to produce art, but she also allows herself leeway. She puts the pieces in place—her paintbrushes out, the sketchbook cracked open—but leaves the next step intentionally less structured. "I'm very motivated by my inner drive. Often I don't have a specific goal in mind as to what the piece will ultimately look like; my emotions and intuitiveness and a drive to get it out are what gets me going."

With a career that has blossomed since she took it into her own hands, Jennifer is an inspiration to anyone who is clock-watching at work, dreaming of holding a paintbrush instead. ✻

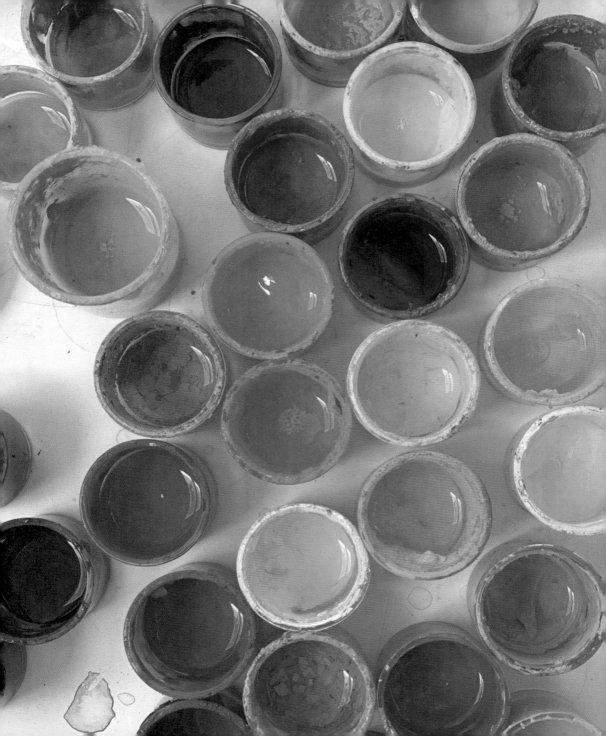

DAILY INSPIRATION

Inspiration comes in many forms: "Big landscapes, travelling, variety in the day-to-day, quiet, many different faces, simple colour combinations, my memory. The small daily things that cross my path," lists Jennifer. By pushing some boundaries, she stays inspired by trying new things: "I do what makes me feel empowered rather than what is expected of me. I try to push through moments of creative block by just putting paint on the paper and mushing it around. That will often spark an idea and get things going." She is, however, often working to commission, and for those projects her process needs to be a bit tighter: "It's a little different when I paint for myself versus a commission. I try to keep the same sense of freedom with projects, but there are more restrictions of course."

"I first need to choose what my subject is. That is usually a quick decision: a bird I saw, a crowd of people, flowers or a landscape." Each choice of subject is drawn from a moment in her day that has made her pause and wonder, slow down, observe and feel peaceful. "My work is about the small moments." She then chooses the medium she wants to work in that day, whether it be gouache, watercolour, pencil or mixed media. "And then I choose a colour plan. Am I going with a warm or cool palette or a limited colour combo? I'm a very intuitive painter and I tend to not make too many plans beyond that. I like to let loose and just paint. Not every piece is successful but that is just part of the process."

augustwren.com
@augustwren

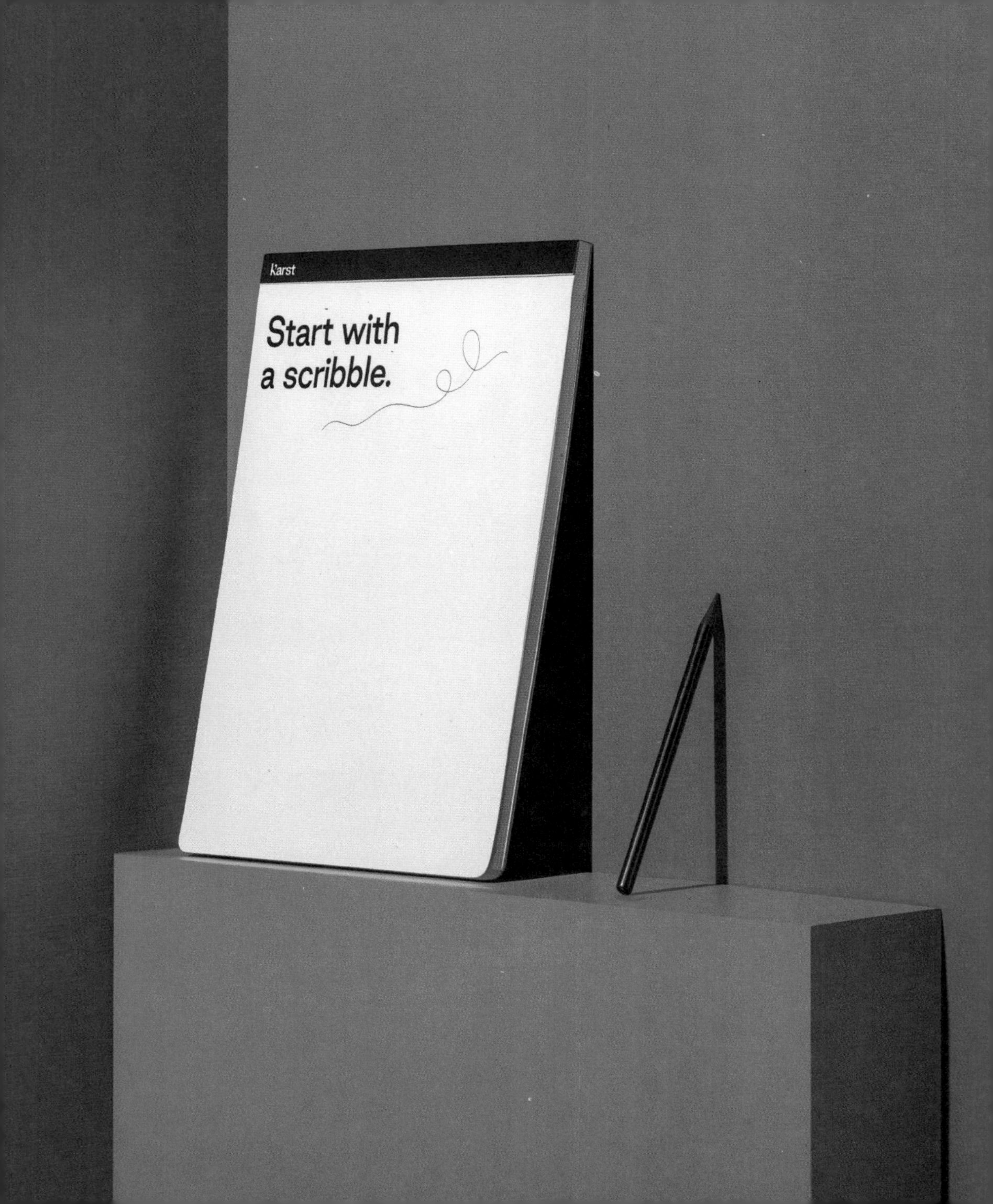
Karst
Start with
a scribble.

KARST

Australian stationery company Karst, founded in 2017 by Kevin Garcia, specializes in notebooks and sketchbooks made of stone paper. They also make lovely "woodless" pencils in graphite and coloured sets, packaged to perfection and ready to impress on your desk.

Kevin discovered stone paper during his travels, where he saw it primarily being used for food packaging because of its waterproof properties. "I have always been the type of person who likes 'life-hacking' stuff, so my mind immediately went toward alternative uses for the technology. And when I learned about the environmental benefits of stone paper, I was even more amazed. The initial idea I had for replacing regular paper with stone paper wore a hole into my brain, and there wasn't anyone in that space yet. So, I decided to take an even deeper plunge into entrepreneurship."

The company name came from the geologist's term "karst landscape"—a terrain that results from the dissolution of soluble rocks such as limestone, marble and gypsum. "The name Karst reflects both our products and our vision—to dissolve, rather, disrupt the paper industry," Kevin explains.

Stone Paper is a sustainable alternative to traditional pulp paper because it uses no trees, water, acids or bleaches in its waste-free production. It is made from reclaimed crushed stone (calcium carbonate) and a resin binder. Unlike traditional paper, it is waterproof, tear-resistant and doesn't suffer from ink bleed-through. It is also brighter than traditional papers and the smooth surface results in friction-free

Woodless Pencils

Just a pencil, minus the wood.

Set of 5

"Our method: challenge assumptions at every stage. Our goal: leave the world better than we found it."

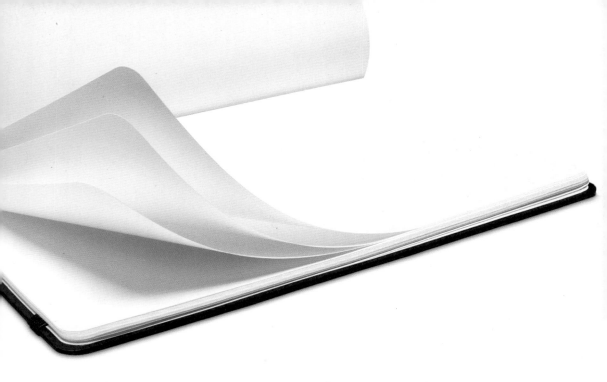

writing. As their marketing copy says, "With no fibre or grain direction, the only friction you'll face when jotting your thoughts down is writer's block."

A companion to their tree-free notebooks are woodless pencils made with a full lead body. With no wooden barrel, you get all the lead and nothing but the lead—five times more than a regular pencil, in fact. The lead or pigment is lightly coated with a matte finish to keep your hands clean. With its handsome black boxes, Karst's packaging is designed to protect while offering a convenient stand from which to select a range of two dozen vibrant colours.

Karst has singled themselves out via their sharp design. Helvetica is not always a typeface one associates with eco-products: "We use rich but not loud colours, authoritative but not messy type, clean lines, and light and shadow in our creative. I knew my business needed to have a very distinct visual and stylistic identity, from a branding point of view." They have notebooks, journals and planners in all sizes and colours, the names of which are evocative: peony, eucalypt, pinot and, of course, stone.

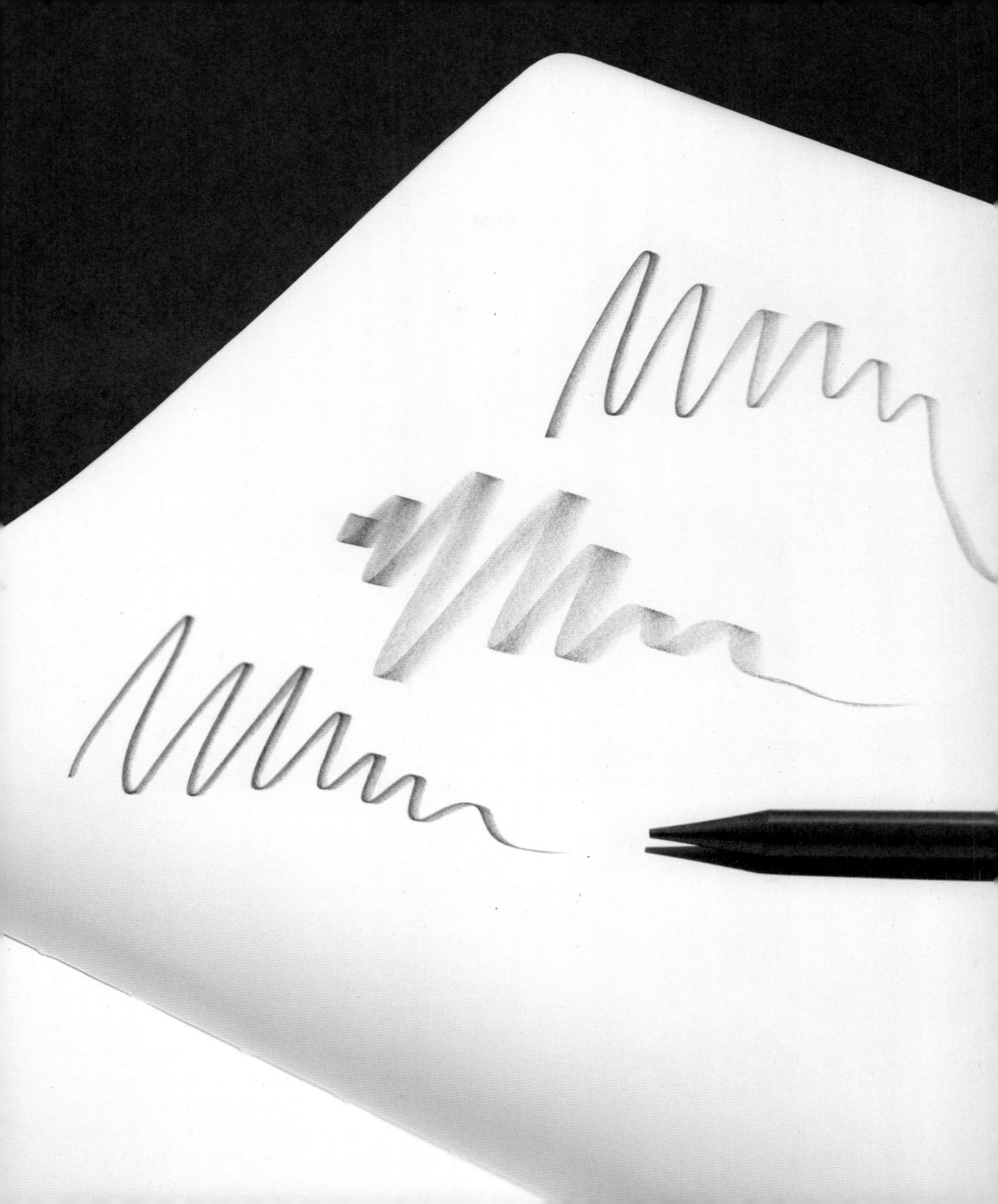

Artist
Pencils

Just a pencil, minus the wood.

Set of
24

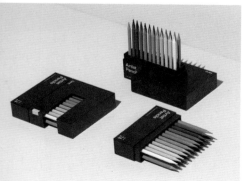

Whilst some might think, erroneously, that any notebook would do the same job, readers of this book will know how untrue that is. As Kevin says: "In a world where every notebook looks more of the same, putting extreme attention to detail is what sets us apart." An example of that is the Karst logo, which has a modified "K" using both serif and sans serif elements: "The 'K' represents another dichotomy, bringing together the old and new—honouring the legacy of fine bookmaking techniques while repurposing them to fit with the needs of today's world." Choosing the right tool for the job is a serious business. And Karst understands this. ✳

"Artists create for the sake of creation. Some art materials are not exactly eco-friendly, like many paints and varnishes. Challenging yourself to use more found materials or create your own mediums is a way to gain a deeper understanding and appreciation for art that goes further than the aesthetic appreciation of it."

SUSTAINABILITY SOLUTIONS

As thoughts of the future of our planet permeate all areas of life, there is consumer awareness and demand for better solutions. Karst believes that the need for a sustainable art paper option is "nearing a tipping point."

Their stone paper is comprised of 80 to 90% crushed stone (calcium carbonate), upcycled waste from construction and mining industries. The remaining 10% is HDPE (high-density polyethylene), a plastic resin that is used to bind the stone particles. "We use a non-virgin and non-toxic HDPE to bind the particles. In Karst Stone Paper, HDPE is found in such small amounts that it leaves no traces of microplastics—HDPE resin oxidizes and is left with no traces. It is also photodegradable which means it breaks down in nature after 6 to 12 months. Think of it as the paper becoming like an egg shell (which is mostly made from calcium carbonate). When Karst Stone Paper fully degrades, there are no microplastics, as the resin oxidises into 1.4 ppm of nitrous oxide and 65 ppm of carbon monoxide, leaving only calcium carbonate behind. Recent research has concluded there are no halogens present."

Karst stone paper uses 60% less energy to

produce than traditional paper. The paper is made in Taiwan in a solar-powered factory. "The finished products are manufactured in China using one of the industry's most experienced suppliers who also supply Moleskine and Montblanc." They also plant a tree for every online purchase and the company is carbon neutral.

Karst is B Corp certified, which means the company meets a specific list of criteria for social and environmental commitments and must be transparent to the public. "Our ultimate purpose has always been to leave the planet better than we found it. From an environmental point of view, that was a no-brainer. But since becoming a B Corp, we've been looking for more ways to have a positive impact for all our stakeholders (customers, employees, local community, society, future generations), through more than our environmental impact."

"By applying the first-principles process to a forward-thinking purpose, we craft beautiful tools that shape our world. Our materials are responsibly sourced, employees are treated and paid fairly, and leaders work for a greater cause than a profit margin. Through our commitment to inspiring people and helping the planet, we take note of what matters. Because what matters today is what shapes tomorrow. We believe tomorrow will be better. But only if we learn from yesterday, and put the work in today."

"Everything we do can leave a carbon footprint. It's important to remember that every single thing we do has an impact on someone or something. There is a need to start thinking in much longer time scales, and we do have more awareness of the impact we have even after we're long gone, whether that's positive or negative."

karststonepaper.com
@karst.stonepaper

KELLEE WYNNE CONRAD

Kellee Wynne Conrad doesn't make slow art: "I take plenty of time to think and absorb the energy around me and then when it's time to act, I do it swiftly. It's the same in life and in my artwork. No slow, meticulous work for me. Art is an *action!*"

Kellee, an artist, author and creative business mentor in Baltimore, grew up around art and worked for many years in the design and craft industry before going full time as a painter and teacher. "Once I decided to make that switch back to painting, I went full speed ahead with my art career. I'm a little bit wild and outspoken and you will find that my art is as well. I love colour and action, so naturally, my work moves quickly, with expressive marks and interesting layers of colour."

When making her own work, Kellee prefers to work with acrylics—painting florals and landscapes in her expressive, abstract style. Her subject matter is often led by courses she is teaching or books she is working on: "Give me layers of mark making and add fields of colour to create lush landscapes, expressive florals or purely non-objective paintings. I am motivated to see the electricity move through me and onto the surface." Kellee prefers to work with a limited palette of art supplies. By limiting her colour choices and focusing on her favourite materials, she has fewer decisions to make. But she also feels this leads to a deeper exploration of the process of making: "The process is far more important to me than the product, and I would say that is the same about my life. I would much rather experience and savour every moment than work tirelessly for title or status."

"Creating is about all the things that words cannot say, which is ironic because I always have a lot to say."

Kellee has recently founded the annual Virtual Art Summit, an online event with contributing professional artists sharing their knowledge in a program that is offered at a pay-what-you-can rate, so everyone can participate. Her colour foundation teaching is also the basis of an "interactive" book, *Mixed Media Color Studio*, and a large parcel of online courses. "I have taught dozens of in-depth art courses over the years that are still available for emerging and established artists. These courses range from oil pastel to mixed media and even my signature abstract florals, but I am most known for my innovative way of using and teaching colour theory so that it really clicks, even for those who have been painting for years."

"I think the most important thing that an artist can learn is that this is a long journey. If you expect to arrive in a year with a fully formed portfolio and know exactly what you want, you will be disappointed. Let it be about the experience along the way and give yourself permission to be imperfect, to make mistakes and to take lots of time to try many different paths. Eventually, the right one will open up to you and you will see everything you have been working towards finally unfold. And I will gladly be here to help you along the way."

Unsurprisingly with all that energy floating around, Kellee multitasks and would never be caught working on just one thing: "I love to have several surfaces going at a time so that my ideas will carry through, especially if I have an 'ah ha' moment and want to see if it's repeatable or how it would turn out in a slightly different way." Recently she has found herself becoming more interested in the mentoring side of her practice, in how artists can earn a living wage from being artists. It can be contentious ground, talking about art and money. Many of us have been taught that being a "proper" artist is a higher calling. But Kellee is having none of that: "Once I realized that I was making a bigger impact with other artists instead of art buyers, I turned my focus to them and began providing the support they needed. Out of that came my ever-growing online business that helps creatives find their voice, create authentic artwork, find their core purpose and build a thriving creative business without the hustle. I have a network of friends and family who give me a tremendous amount of support. But most of this path I have had to figure out myself." ✳

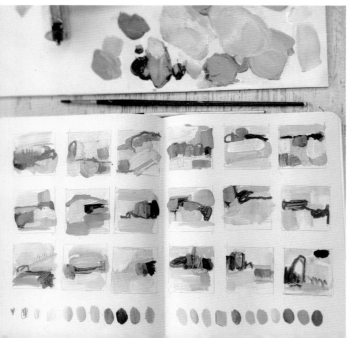

LIMITS AND LAYERS

Kellee loves acrylic paint, water-soluble graphites, oil pastels and Stonehenge paper: "If I only had a few things to work with, those would be my primary materials." Over recent years, she has limited her colour palette, which has, in turn, bolstered her art practice. Not only does limiting supplies reduce the time spent making decisions, it has helped her create more harmonious artwork: "My design sense has more focus with fewer choices. I love layers, and while sometimes you will find me leaving a fresh mark raw on the canvas, often my process is about adding layer after layer of mark making, collage, paint and more mark making so that you can see all the parts of the process peeking through at the end." One of her favourite tools to paint with, besides a brush, is a brayer—a small roller used to apply paint. She loves the layers and transparency you can obtain with it. And the brayer gives unexpected textures every time: "I'm a big fan of anything else that leaves an interesting texture as well: stencils, stamps, found objects, old brushes. Anything goes if it means I can create from a place of curiosity."

WHAT INSPIRES KELLEE

"Life. The way the shadow falls across the living room floor. The peeling paint on an old sign. A sock left on the stairs. The sound of the cicadas. The stars on a dark night. The laugh of my kids. A moment of undefined spiritual connection. A plastic bag stuck in the tree. The smell of basil. The painful goodbye of a beloved pet. Paris. You. Shall I go on? As you can see, everything inspires me. Everything. Once I opened my heart to gratitude and mindfulness, everything became a beautiful possibility of expression. My mind never rests from making all the connections that life has given us. I'm not always motivated to make art, but I am always inspired."

kelleewynnestudios.com
@kelleewynnestudios

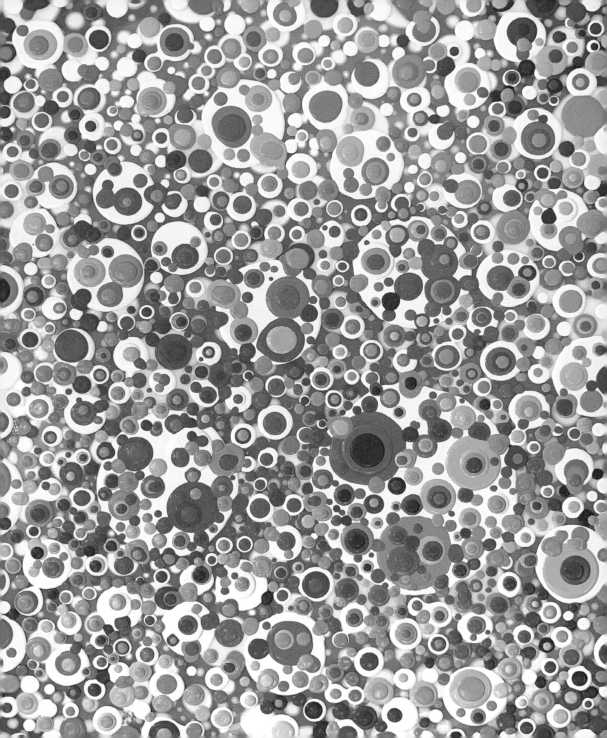

KIMBERLY BLACKSTOCK

For those of us who love art supplies—and, in particular, paint—there is something very satisfying about seeing the paint as a living, flowing, textured entity. Artist Kimberly Blackstock uses acrylic paints and pouring mediums to bring extra dimension to her art: "My most recent work is playful. I use welcoming colours, drawing the viewer in, while the textures open the door for further exploration. It's not difficult to visualize running your fingers along the dried paint and imagine what the sensations of these raised surfaces might feel like."

She uses pouring medium, a liquid that is mixed with acrylic paint, expanding the potential of the paint by turning it into fluid colour that can be applied with a squeeze bottle. Kimberly's paintings are a celebration of the properties and fluidity of acrylic paint. Outlines and details merge together, swirling like the inside of a glass marble. Piped icing lines of paint streak across a canvas. And dots are dripped in confetti-like abundance. She has, she says, "a strong dedication to exploring and pushing the boundaries of paint application."

Kimberly's process is fairly intuitive—new ideas are on a continual conveyer belt in her head: "I can create a clearer visual there than on paper. Once a vision drives me, I work out the process and create a colour palette. If pouring paint, I mix for days until I have about 90% of what I need. The paint needs to be the right viscosity. I continually add small increments of acrylic and medium whilst shaking and de-clogging the bottles. It is a messy job—I get paint everywhere despite all precautions taken." She was not always an acrylic woman; she preferred oils the first few years of

"With a strong dedication to explore and push the boundaries of paint application, the intent of my work is to stimulate action with the viewer as a form of communication and to invoke a desire to involve senses beyond just sight."

her art career: "I painted more representationally and loved how they blend and stay wet longer. It wasn't until I had children that I felt I needed to switch to acrylic. I was concerned about their health and the way I was using oils because my art space was intertwined with our living space much more at that point. I still prefer oils for representational work but acrylics are much more versatile for the exploratory work."

Playing to the quirks and properties of her chosen art materials, Kimberly has developed a meticulous process, allowing the dots or lines of paint to dry between layers. She does not want random blending between them. "I often wonder who else would bother doing this," she says. "My 'dot paintings' have painted layers, resin layers and then many extra layers of poured dots. I can only put so many dots down at a time or they will all join together. It is the same with my linear line 'drips.' I calculate where the drips will go with each passing, so they don't touch each other when still wet. When dry, I flip the art upside down and repeat over and over until I am content with the outcome." Depending on the piece, some works can take a very long time to make. It is not uncommon for a painting to require 25 to 30 days of application, with many days of drying time in between. "If the dots are large I have to let them dry a lot longer before applying paint or resin on top; small dots might only need a day before I can apply more paint," Kimberly explains. "Other works might only take 4 or 10 days of application, with dry times in between. This is why I tend to work on multiple pieces at a time."

Educated in graphic design and illustration, Kimberly juggled painting on the side for many years before it came to the forefront. "I figured out exactly where I was supposed to be," she says. She taught visual arts at her community art centre and in public schools in Greater Vancouver for over 10 years, which helped her build networks to support her when it came time to paint: "Building the relationship with my

BLACK STOCK

"As creative beings it should be easier to figure out ways to reuse and repurpose. So let's challenge ourselves to do just that."

community, and having them see my commitment and passion for what I do, created referrals: a natural, organic word-of-mouth growth and connection to a wider audience. Galleries and the film industry (using my paintings as props) have, without a doubt, also played a big role in furthering a connection to a network of people I may not have normally come in contact with. All four of these—my community, the galleries, the film industry and most definitely social media—have intertwined and supported ongoing audience interest in my work." She admits to being a bit shy and has never felt comfortable with public speaking. But through her art she feels able to speak confidently: "My work has connected me with many people and I love this form of communication that brings us together."

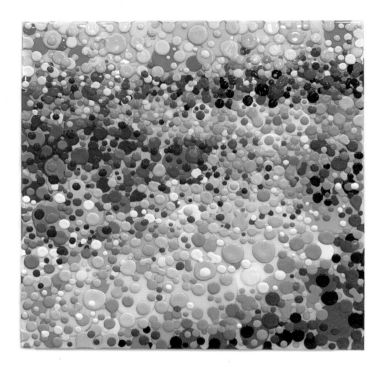

Finding inspiration comes fairly easily to Kimberly. Indeed, she has a backlog of ideas at any one time. She is lucky that she has never experienced artist's block. On the contrary, she doesn't have enough time to create everything that is flying around in her head: "In that sense my imagination provides great inspiration to my life as an artist. I am also very much inspired by my natural surroundings; the West Coast is a theme I've been exploring for the past two years. I think it is important to paint what you are passionate about so you can tell a story directly from your heart." Kimberly seems to be an artist content with herself, as a person and as an artist: "I would describe my aesthetic as being uplifting and free, however at the same time a little complicated—not in a suffering way, but a way that makes people question or engage a bit more in an inquiring manner. Most of my work is multi-layered and the applications are a little unusual or unconventional. I'd say I am a bit like my work in that sense." ✳

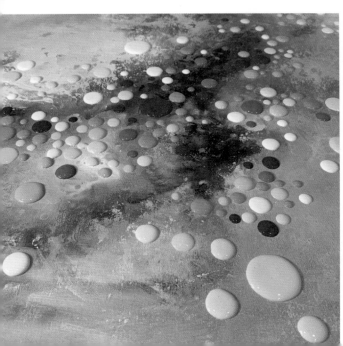

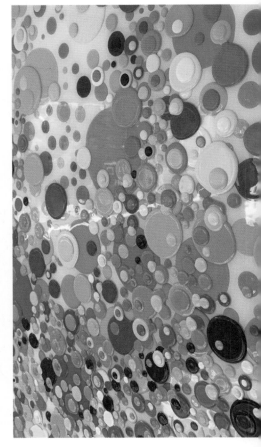

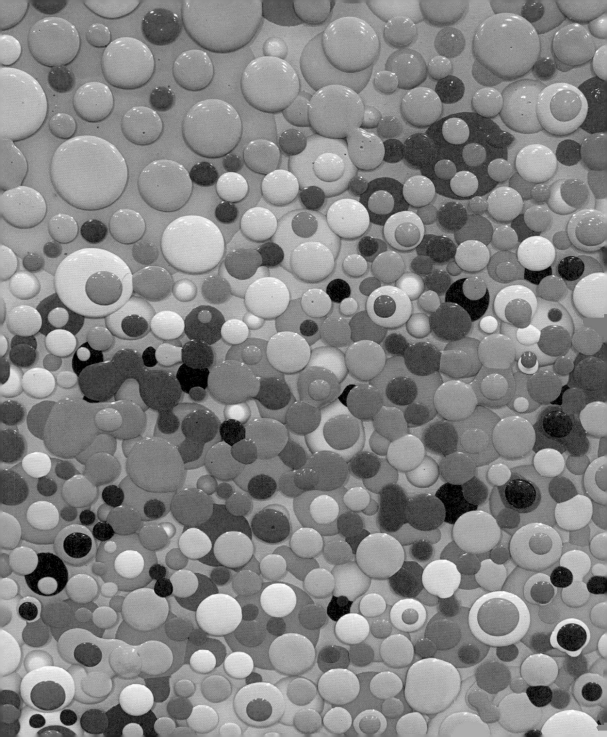

CAN'T LIVE WITHOUT

Kimberly encourages playful exploration when it comes to new techniques and supplies: "Understanding multiple mediums and techniques, and taking the time to learn how to use them successfully, really opens doors to being able to express your vision the way you really want it to be seen." However, the two materials she couldn't live without are acrylic paint and pouring medium. "Acrylic is amazingly versatile and fun, it is very forgiving and inviting for experimentation, it's wonderful for incorporating into mixed-media paintings, whether realistic or abstract. And then, pouring medium not only lets me explore acrylic application further, it gives that tactile 'touch me' interactive feel that I love having the viewer engage with, even if it is just with their eyes and imagination." Her favourite creative tools are squeeze bottles: lots and lots of them. And of course her hands: "My hands in particular are so multifunctional, and unlike all my other supplies, they are always right where I left them. They truly are the best!"

kimberlyblackstock.com
@blackstockpaint

KREMER PIGMENTS

Kremer Pigments are made in an old converted 18th-century flour mill (now known as the Colour Mill) in Aichstetten, Germany. The company was founded in 1977 by Georg Kremer, a chemist with a special interest in history. As a graduate student, he had started making pigments using historical methods, at the request of conservator friends who could not source what they needed. Within a few years, he was supplying a colourful compendium of over 100 pigments to conservators, painters, makers and artisans from his shops in Munich (opened 1982) and New York (opened in 1990).

Today there is more interest in art supply products and processes than ever before. A lot of artists who have been painting for decades never learned how to make their own paint—or even what their paint was actually made of. Suppliers like Kremer are changing that. Kremer Pigments NYC now sells over a thousand unique products: pigments and ingredients for fine art, art conservation and restoration. They are also used in traditional artisanal crafts like violin making, making natural dyes and gilding.

Roger Danilo Carmona has worked at Kremer Pigments NYC since 2007. In his personal art practice, everything he uses is from scratch, even gesso: "It truly transformed my relationship with my work. I try to share this paint-making knowledge and experience with our customers." Nearly all of the people who have worked in the NYC shop over the years have been practicing artists or future art conservators.

"By making their own paints and choosing each ingredient, an artist becomes more acutely aware of their own process. When you make your own paints, you can conserve materials and control waste."

Walking into the NYC shop, you see hundreds of colours lining the shelves. The options can be overwhelming: "It used to be that customers coming into Kremer were professionals who knew exactly what they needed and didn't ask for any direction," Roger says. "However, as we gained a wider audience, we found that a lot of new customers had a high level of interest but lacked practical training." In a specialized shop, the staff are as important as the products. As Roger explains: "You can make it as simple or as complex as you like. You can start small, with one or two new ingredients and build on that. The more you work with pigments and raw materials, the more you learn." Staff take their time speaking with each customer in order to learn about and understand their process. Then they make informed recommendations.

Making your own art supplies has the added benefit of knowing exactly what is in them. You can make supplies without the use of preservative chemicals, animal products or synthetic pigments, for example. You can also conserve materials and control waste by making just a small batch. "Using raw materials will open up new possibilities to any artist, no matter what their work is like," says Roger. "Understanding your materials gives you the liberty to play confidently with them and explore new ideas. A great advantage of using pigments is that you can use the same jar of pigment to make any kind of paint."

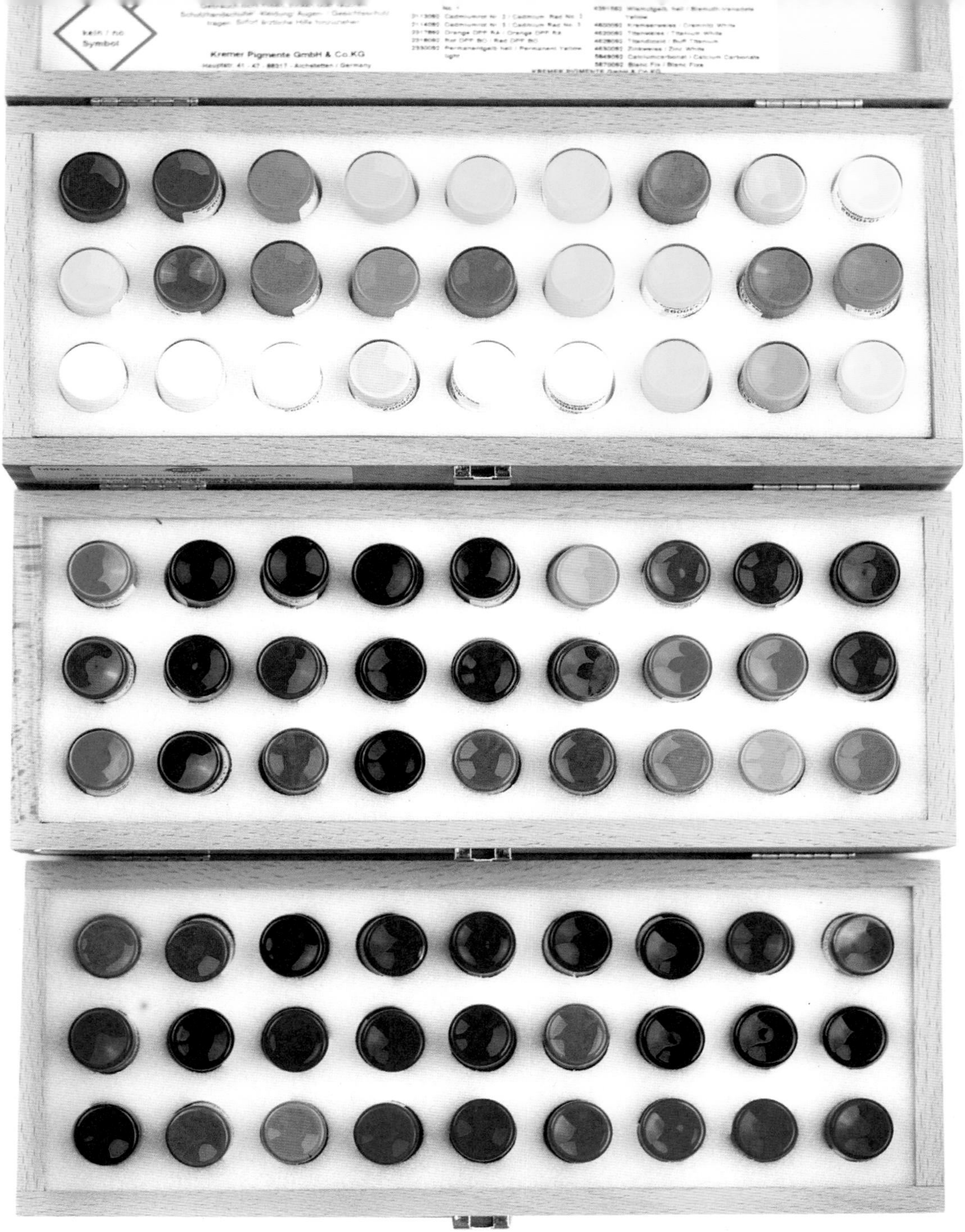
kein / no
Symbol
Kremer Pigmente GmbH & Co.KG

Kremer uses historical recipes and methods that have stood the test of time, while incorporating modern ingredients and methods where they serve well. For example, their inks are made of traditional "shellac soap," which dries semi-gloss and is water resistant. But they are made with modern synthetic pigments, not dyes, so they are highly saturated and will not fade. Oil paints are made using only pure pigment ground in linseed oil.

One of the most popular Kremer products is their conservation-quality watercolours, made of pure pigment, gum arabic binder and no fillers—just small pans of pure colour. Roger explains: "Dr. Kremer developed a proprietary recipe for our watercolour binder which has proved to make paints of luxurious consistency. The honey and glycerin in it keep the pans a bit tacky, so the colour picks up beautifully on the brush. The intensity is hard to believe until you actually paint with them. The character of each pigment sings when used in watercolour." As well as wondrous pigments and singing watercolours, Kremer Pigments NYC offers other interesting raw materials for making paint, varnishes and many other art supply goodies: "We think of our shop like a grocery store, where each ingredient has the potential to be used in a multitude of recipes." ✳

FROM FRESCOS TO FRAMES

If you have been to a major museum, you have probably seen Kremer products at work—perhaps in a large contemporary painting that was made with vast quantities of sloshed paint, or in the almost-invisible restoration of a crumbling fresco painting, with patched-up gods and putti, or in the burnished gilding of a frame that holds your favourite portrait in a museum. Kremer Pigments are known, especially, for their use in traditional egg tempera icon paintings.

Even "non-artists" use Kremer products, for projects like painting a home in a custom-tinted lime paint, or refinishing cabinets with a coating of mica paint. The sealing of a handmade wooden canoe can be done with their asphaltum, or you can add their pigments to polyurethane floor coatings. "There are dozens of ways to use each product," says Roger, "so we generally do not dictate specific instructions." The Kremer website does offer extensive information and instructions for paint recipes and methods.

RAW MATERIALS

Most of Kremer's earth pigments and chalks are sourced from quarries all over the world: lapis lazuli from Afghanistan and Chile, cavansite from India, cinnabar from China and meteorite brown from Morocco. There is literally a world of colour behind their shop door.

"Everything you see in our NYC shop was measured, mixed or bottled in our colour mill in Aichstetten, where our 250 house-milled pigments and our 100-plus handmade watercolours, varnishes, oil paints and inks are still made," says Roger. "We have an old stone mill which is still used for grinding some of our pigments that are sensitive to the heat of modern machines. For most pigments, though, a modern mill is used."

kremerpigments.com
@kremerpigmentsnyc

SAFETY

Since they offer the raw materials used in making paints and varnishes, Kremer's labelling is based on delivering scientific information such as particle size, chemical composition, materials suitability, historical background and safety precautions for using fine particles and potential chemicals with various toxicities. As pretty as the colours might be, many pigments can be dangerous. Being educated about a particular pigment and exercising caution are necessary when mixing one's own art supplies—any fine dust is harmful if inhaled or if it gets in the eyes, for example. Solvents and oils are combustible. One should never eat or drink in the presence of pigments and solvents. Always wash your hands after any contact. Raw materials and supplies should always be kept out of the reach of children and pets.

Kremer provides safety data for each pigment. Lapis lazuli, a bright blue from South America, is deemed to be a non-toxic or hazardous substance, whereas green raw umber requires the purchaser to complete a hazardous item disclaimer, since this pigment may contain lead. Many pigments are carcinogenic, such as bright cadmium yellow. Dark blue cobalt requires protective gloves and eyewear, and can only be sold to professional users, as it may cause allergic skin reactions, and contaminated clothing should not be allowed out of the workplace.

Safe handling procedures, including respirators, protective clothing and ventilation, are extremely important, and raw pigments and solvents should only be used by those over 21 years of age. Many pigments are not intended for home use.

LA MAISON DU PASTEL

La Maison du Pastel in Paris, founded in 1720, is the world's oldest pastel manufacturer. By hand, La Maison du Pastel makes sumptuous soft pastels that carry the name of Henri Roché, the chemist-pharmacist who took over the business in 1880. The company is still family owned—by Isabelle Roché, who runs it with Margaret Zayer. In such a small team, roles are many and various and often shared. Isabelle took over the company, which was being run by her distant cousins, sisters Denise and Gisèle Roché (both then in their eighties), in 2000. She ran it on her own for a decade, doing everything—until, in 2010, Margaret visited for a summer placement and never left.

The two women run the company's historical shop in Paris—a true art supply destination shop. It has been in its current location since 1912 and, thankfully, a lot of the original character and art magic is still there. The shop is lined with shelf after shelf of old wooden trays, hand-labelled with the number and name of each pastel (G6581 Vert Meleze, 6121 Vert Japon, 8281 Violet très rouse...), all waiting to be pulled out by knowledgeable staff and shown off to eager artists. They also sell their pastels through two other specialist stores: Sennelier in Paris and Rochester Art Supply in New York. Their pastels have been serving the artist community for a long time, as Margaret explains: "Henri Roché retained the old company's artisanal 18th-century pastel production techniques but reimagined the recipes to create a product that responded to the needs of the artists of the era, such as Degas, Whistler, Legros and Chéret. The result has

"Our pastels work as an extension of an artist's creative vision, quite literally delivering on paper the ideas and feelings that course through their fingertips."

found its way into the hands of great artists of each generation that's followed."

As well as being the oldest pastel manufacturer, their colour range is also the largest in the world. "Our pastels are essentially made from powdered pigments that we source worldwide, primarily from Europe or North America. Many of our earth pigments are still quarried in the south of France," says Margaret. Each delicate pastel is made in the traditional way: "They are made in a workshop in an old farm complex in the French countryside. And they are still made entirely by hand at every step of the process, using just a few simple tools to facilitate things: antique scales, wood planks, basins, spatulas, an old book press... Our process remains entirely traditional because those are the methods that produce the best result for us."

The joy of a product well made and simply packaged is central to the longevity of the brand. La Maison du Pastel pastels are known for their unique characteristics: remarkably intense colours and firm, dry and slightly gritty texture. These qualities make them suitable for drawing both controlled lines and softer, subtle, shimmering layers. Roché pastels (all 1,650 colour options) are separated into families of nine different gradations: colours mixed with white, mixed with black or crossed with another colour. The rich reds, the exceptionally dark 9181 Extra Black (the world's darkest black pastel) and the metallic and iridescent colours (like 9640 Scarab and 9441 Diamond White) have proved particularly popular in the last few years.

As visual people, we want our art supplies to surpass the basic function of mark making and also to supply us with beauty and inspiration. La Maison du Pastel's creations are exceptional at meeting these demands. Oh, the joy of choosing from a never-ending rainbow of pastel shades (and of every shade within those shades)—each one wrapped in a paper bearing the name of a 19th-century family. And to buy your pastel selection nestled in a wooden box with a clasp? Just the very idea provokes an urgent need. ✳

HOW TO MAKE A PASTEL

The process behind making any pastel comes down to three things: pigment, binder and shaping. La Maison du Pastel pastels start their lives with a careful sourcing of fine pigments and an (often prolonged) stage of formulation to work out how best to put those pigments to use. Once a formula is approved, a colour takes life when its pigments and binder (a closely guarded house secret) are weighed, wetted and put through a vintage mechanical grinder to be mixed.

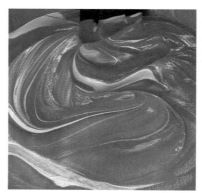

The colour tints and shades are determined by eye. Both the colour in question and the required tinting or shading colour (white, black or other) are then blended in different proportions to achieve the grada-tion desired. The resulting blends—still fluid pastes—are then put in a cloth and the water is then manually squeezed out of them under an old book press, towards achieving a suitable texture for rolling out. The paste is then individually weighed and made into sticks by hand. These are then cut to size and stamped with the Maison's signature ROC (for Roché) before air drying for several weeks.

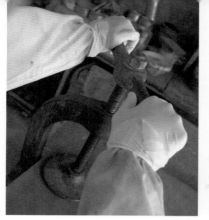

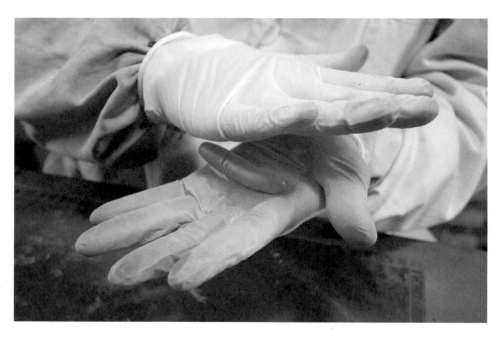

"Less is more when it comes to our packaging and branding. We like for our colours to speak for themselves in the simplest, most harmonious way possible within their surroundings."

2531. Rouge carmin | T. 2551. Rose clair

SM

T. 2611. Rouge grenat | G. 2721. Rouge carnation

MAGASINS

LADARA MCKINNON

LaDara McKinnon's abstract paintings are each a force of nature, full of movement, colour and life. "My personality is reflected in what I make through expressive mark making, loose brush strokes and the level of care and technique that goes into each painting," she says. LaDara grew up in Hawaii and Japan, where her love for art began. Her parents knew early on that she was artistically inclined and allowed her to explore her creativity as she would. She was part of a military family and through travel was exposed to cultures that celebrated vivid colours found in nature and the environment. "I am most inspired by nature. The sky, to me, often looks like abstract paintings and the natural colour palette is my favourite to work with. I do smaller studies that keep me coming up with new ideas. And I often find myself inspired by new words that I come across that you'll find as the names of my paintings."

From her studio in Charlotte, North Carolina, LaDara paints with her canvas hung on the wall. She prefers standing when painting rather than sitting at an easel or desk. This comes as no surprise when you see the moves she makes with her paintbrush on her canvas. Her studio is filled with large windows to let in lots of light, which also benefits the plants on the window ledge. "I have a wood-topped rolling cart that holds the supplies that I am currently working with and stores additional supplies underneath. The other walls in my studio display my vision board, positive reminders for motivation and inspiration. And I always have candles and earphones nearby, so that I can create a calm space when I am working."

"I would describe my aesthetic as expressive, organic and free flowing. It has a sense of softness and rawness that collides in a beautiful way. It almost feels like visual poetry."

Her preferred medium is professional-grade acrylic paints; they are versatile and easy to manipulate. She uses high-quality wrapped canvas and a variety of brands of brushes, with a preference for flat head brushes (so she can make marks without pressing too hard on the canvas). Her use of flat head brushes comes from having also learned to paint with oils. She uses gloss varnishes and gel mediums, the latter used to thicken paint so that it shows up marks and brush strokes. Her favourite tool to make those marks is a simple wooden skewer: "I love using skewers because they allow me to carve into the canvas for mark making, which is a staple in my work."

Abstract art is where LaDara's artistic passions play out. She responds to the emotional connection it creates between herself and others. Much of her work is done on commission, for which LaDara works with clients to agree on palettes and approaches, needs and potential inspirations. The rest of the conversation happens on her canvas: "I have always loved and experienced art and colour in a way that allowed me to express emotions that I couldn't always articulate. Through my art, I am able to take time for myself, whilst helping others to express themselves."

She hopes her abstract art reflects back something intrinsic to the person looking at it—that a connection is made. "I want each viewer to feel free, similar to the feeling you get when you stick your hand out a moving car window. I want people to see their stories in my work and their personalities reflected back. ✳

"There are two ways that I figure out when a painting is finished: first is the intuitive process; it is like an inner exhale. The technical way, secondly, is making sure that the principles of fine art can be found, such as value, contrast and composition."

FROM PAINT TO PAINTING

Acrylic paints are very versatile. They can be blended with other mediums, are fast drying and are non-toxic—all qualities that encourage creative exploration with colour theory, layering and texture. When inspiration strikes, LaDara starts with mixing colours. "I select the colours that support the feeling that I want to express in the end result," she says. "I am always sure to add pops of colour, like neon orange and fluorescent pink."

The first layer of paint is applied intuitively. "I add in either warm or cool colours first and then I start to add the remaining colours of the colour palette into the work. I am mindful to create contrast and then begin to consider the composition for the next layer." At this point, it is usually time for LaDara to step away. "I usually take a break to meditate on the piece, which could be from two days to three weeks, by putting the paintings away."

When viewing the work in progress at a later date, her perspective is fresh and she can better adjudicate what needs to be added or subtracted. "Then I add little details like pops of colours, mark making and highlights to create the finished look. This last step is what I think really makes the painting appeal to the viewer and helps them discover new areas of interest within the piece."

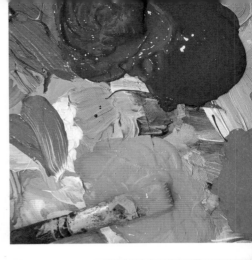

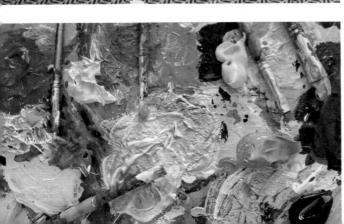

IT'S ALL IN THE TECHNIQUE

LaDara lists the methods used in her art-making: subtraction, engraving, layering, mark making, heavy or thick paint and loose movement. Subtraction is the process of removing a layer by scraping the paint off or painting white over areas of the painting, especially areas that she is no longer in love with. Conversely, "subtracting also involves removing some of the areas of the painting that I am in love with so that they don't hold me back from obtaining the end result." For LaDara, mark making means "freely making brushstrokes on the canvas." And engraving is the process of carving into wet paint. Layering is the process of overlapping a layer of wet paint on top of an already dry painting. Heavy or thick paint is a specific type or consistency of paint that provides texture on the canvas. And loose movement is "a brushstroke where you are holding the brush and letting the brush stroke as freely as possible with as little control as possible."

ladaramckinnon.com
@ladarafineart

LESLIE ROTTNER

Leslie Rottner creates art with natural brushes she makes herself, a creative process that happened purely by chance. "I wanted to make some fun marks," she recalls. "I use found sticks and repurposed vintage paintbrushes, brooms and feathers to make the brush tops." The first designs were very rustic, but she soon developed a love for beautiful found wood. "The brush tops are still a bit unruly but the handles are a little nicer." More like small sculptures than any traditional expectation of what a brush should be, they are visceral and challenge what we think of as "proper" art supplies. "The brushes I make are made for one purpose, and that is to create marks with rustic materials and to encourage playful exploration."

This notion of playful exploration can be traced to Leslie's childhood. "My creative path began at a very young age when I realized that I could have an idea and bring that idea to life with my own hands. That concept was very powerful to me and I still feel that way today. To create something with my hands and use it, gift it or send it out in the world is not only fulfilling but thrilling."

Leslie is inspired by her natural surroundings. She lives in Lake Placid, a village in the Adirondack Mountains in Upstate New York. "My studio is my little slice of heaven in a converted part of our house," she says. She has lovely shelves of interesting things to look at whilst she works, hunks of interesting wood, baskets of strings and other items, and feathers she has found: "I love being surrounded with things that inspire me and prompt me to delve into an idea. I have collections

"What I create allows me the freedom of managing small portions of disorder and chance. When I think of my personality, there is a threshold where those things become overwhelming and too much. But in my creative practice, the chaos is manageable."

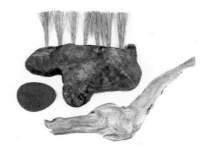

of natural things that are beautiful to look at but also continue to remind me how awesome Mother Nature is." When working on the brushes she does most of the dirty work in the garage, which is also her husband's woodshop. There she has access to the bandsaw, sanders and drill press. She does the finishing work in her studio.

A brush begins with finding the right stick. "I want it to be functional and beautiful, and it has to feel good in your hand. Finding a beat-up old stick and uncovering what is underneath the bark is one of my favourite steps in the process." Leslie certainly lives in the right place for scavenging her materials. Repurposing and recycling are important to her practice and she knows this has a positive impact on the environment: "I reuse as much and as often as possible. I repurpose brushes and brooms that might be tossed into the garbage and the sticks are just found." The hidden beauty of each stick shows once she has cleaned it up, and sanded, oiled and waxed it. Leslie searches for wood with interesting shapes and imperfections, and some require more work than others to make them shine. Whilst the handles of her brushes are made from found cedar, and sometimes antlers, the brush tops are made

"Sharing materials that you no longer use with other artists or having an artist's tag sale is a great way to give materials a longer life and not have them end up in landfills."

from recycled vintage paint brushes, brooms, masonry brushes and feathers: "If I'm lucky I find the brush material at estate sales or thrift shops. If I don't have luck there then I find them on eBay or Etsy."

Leslie's collages are also formed around found materials that may otherwise have ended up in the trash and landfills. She layers vintage papers, old books, type and ephemera to pull together visual narratives and surreal collections. You can imagine they might once have formed someone's personal effects. Her collages are very often anchored by a scrap of found writing, a number, a cut-out postage mark: "As a self-taught artist, I use an intuitive and thoughtful approach to transform often overlooked materials into a new visual story."

Having two different pursuits, brushes and collage, allows her mind to rest from one while working on the other: "This allows me to have fresh eyes and perspective while continuing with a creative practice." The one-of-a-kind brushes can be purchased individually or by subscription. And, really, could anything be nicer than getting a beautiful sculptural art brush posted to you every few months? ✳

MAKING AN ART BRUSH

Leslie's brush-making process is a labour of love. For the most part, she hunts for sticks that look solid, without any soft spots. At this point, she needs to be able to see something in the shape, something that she can evolve. If the sticks are damp after she gets them back to her studio, she dries them out before using them. Dirt or debris comes off, then the bark comes off, too. Using a bandsaw, Leslie cuts them to the desired size and then sands them: "In most cases, the sanding part takes the longest."

After sanding, the pieces are "cooked" in a 200°F oven for three to four hours. This is a practical and important step. "The internal temperature needs to be 130°F to take care of any possible insects," she explains. After cooling, the brush handles are coated with hemp oil, and then waxed once the hemp oil is dry. Sometimes she adds embellishments like leather or leaves curling around the handle, made with a woodburning tool. The top is drilled with one or more holes, depending on the size, and the brush material—recycled from old brushes and brooms—is put in the hole: "Once dry I trim up the brush, make sure the bristles are not falling out, check the handle and lastly wood burn my initials in the bottom."

leslierottnerart.com
@leslierottnerart

LIQUITEX

The Permanent Pigments Company, a small, family-owned business for milling artist's oil colours, was founded in 1933 in Cincinnati, Ohio, by Henry Levison, an American colour chemist. In 1955 Levison renamed his company Liquitex, after his latest product: the first acrylic gesso. The name was a blend of the words "liquid" and "texture," and with their new name the company sounded much more scientific and future-focused. As Levison said at the time: "I'm only happy when I'm trying to create something new." In 1956 he and Liquitex launched the first water-based acrylic paint. Liquitex also began organizing artist show-and-tells around this time, working with artist Garo Antreasian to road test Liquitex colours whilst he painted a mural commission at Ohio University. Back then it was a new and savvy way to market art supplies and a forerunner of the artist collaborations, tie-ins and promotions we are so used to today.

Before 1956, oils, watercolours and solvent-based acrylics were the only paint choices for artists. The new acrylic that Liquitex was selling was somewhere between an oil and a watercolour paint. It could be used on most surfaces, it dried quickly and could be cleaned up with water, and it worked in a range of viscosities and was durable. Spirit-based acrylic paints were first developed in the 1940s as house paints, and only later taken up by artists. In 1965, in order to break his paints into the art market, Levison started a program of show-and-tells called the Liquitex Lecture Demonstration Program. It was the first artist-to-artist program in colleges and universities in the USA. In

the year 2000, Liquitex became part of Colart International Holdings, a company that also owns heritage art supply brands including Winsor & Newton (founded in 1832), Lefranc Bourgeois (founded in 1720) and Conté à Paris (founded in 1795).

Liquitex still makes the Soft Body Acrylic that was the original formulation back in 1956—in a nice new bottle and in 94 colours. It is a low-viscosity acrylic paint giving "excellent coverage, a satin finish and high levels of artist-quality pigment for archival brilliance." And they now make Heavy Body Acrylic too. Each of their paints comes in a squeezy tube containing a thick and high-viscosity, pigment-rich colour, providing "crisp brush strokes and knife marks," suitable for painters looking for impasto and texture.

"A collaborative team of artists, product development specialists and acrylics chemists work together on new concepts for formulations, formats, colours and supporting tools," says Liquitex regarding its

ARTIST MEKIA MACHINE, JUST IMAGINE RESIDENCY

product development. "A project can take anything from weeks to years to complete, depending on the brief and complexity: our new Acrylic Gouache took over two years to develop." In a special restricted access room, all aspects of the product are tested for light-fastness, opacity, stability and colour intensity. "When the formulation has passed all the lab tests, it's handed over to the research and development team at one of our factories to scale up. We then start a production trial to make sure that when it's made in bulk amounts, the formulation will deliver the same quality performance."

By the 1980s, acrylic paints had become an almost ubiquitous art supply, used by many artists, and this remains the case today. Many of the artists and makers in this book love acrylic paints for their ease of use and their dependable, as well as their zingy, non-fading colours that will remain bright and dazzling for many years. ✳

WHAT IS ACRYLIC PAINT?

Acrylic paint is a fast-drying paint made of pigment suspended in acrylic polymer emulsion and plasticizers with silicone oils, defoamers, stabilizers or metal soaps. Liquitex acrylic paint is made of three things: a pigment, an emulsion and a binder. The pigment is the coloured bit—a dry, powdery material that does not dissolve and remains suspended when mixed with acrylic polymer emulsion. According to Liquitex, "pigments can be organic, inorganic, natural and synthetic. They have little or no affinity for the surface to which they are applied." The emulsion is a combination of water and acrylic polymer, which creates a polymer emulsion. "Once the water leaves the system via evaporation or absorbtion, the paint dries, creating a stable clear polymer film full of trapped coloured pigment particles." And a binder is an acrylic polymer without the water. The binder gives paint its handling characteristics and durability. Acrylic colours dry as a result of water evaporation.

liquitex.com
@liquitexofficial

MEGAN WOODARD JOHNSON

Megan Woodard Johnson originally trained to be a graphic designer, but making art and design on a screen wasn't for her. "I found that I love the art of design but withered in the computer lab. I couldn't pursue a career where my creativity would need to be executed on screen. If my hands aren't touching materials, my ideas dry up." After graduating with a BFA in graphic design, she veered off the art and design path into project management and event planning, learning skills she is now glad to have. But whilst creativity was part of her life, art was not. Then, in 2007, "I looked up and realized that through work, marriage and parenthood, it had been over a decade since I'd identified myself as an artist. So, I began to reclaim that role."

In West Bend, Wisconsin, Megan makes abstract, mixed-media paintings, using collage and paint to great effect. Her paintings are deeply layered with art supplies and meaning. She begins her works by completely covering her substrate (typically heavy paper or a birch panel) with collage, much of which comes from vintage paper and ephemera. The collage layer is left to dry overnight before being sealed with acrylic matte medium to protect the paper from the oncoming paint. After that come many layers of gestural lines made of oil pastel, coloured pencil, graphite and sometimes ink. And big, loose areas of acrylic paint. At this point Megan is working intuitively: "I don't worry too much yet about specific composition or colour choices. Eventually,

"My art is made to pull the viewer in to engage in everyday but authentic conversation. Sometimes that conversation is with me, but the best is when it's with themselves."

though, I get to a point where the composition seems to emerge, and a colour palette settles in."

She will now begin to work more slowly and consider her next changes carefully: "I add more paint and marks, and begin bringing more collage into play. This time I choose pieces that play a role in the composition. Colour and pattern are important and placement is important." This second collage layer provides new colours, hard edges and pattered contrast to the gestural marks she has made. All these layers allow for different readings of the finished piece: "Some details are recognizable and pull specific memories to the surface but often there's more of a recognition of the overall depth and detail of regular life. I'm motivated to connect people with memories and connections that feel personal and universal at once."

Megan is a stickler for well-made, quality materials. She wants her art supplies, from the substrates to the paint, to the hanging hardware, to be of good quality and stand the test of time: "My paintbrushes are my favourite tools. Aside from loving how different brushes can make so many different types of marks—swoops and blobs, drips and smudges—my brushes represent my growth as an artist. I used to paint quite carefully, and very small. As my ideas grew, the size of my work grew, and the variety and size of my

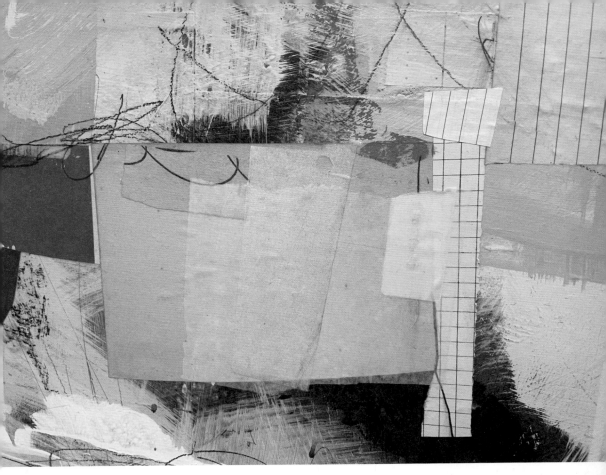

brushes grew. I'll be honest, I abuse them. And I often use the 'wrong' kind. But they do exactly what I want."

Megan describes her art career as a "slow and steady" story. She started with a tiny studio space in the corner of the basement and the time she could find to paint during unreliable toddler naps: "Step by step I built my voice, and my work grew. I hired a babysitter for one afternoon a week so I could have a longer period of time to focus. It took over a year to be in this studio, doing this level of work." She knows people have been a deciding factor in her story. In the early years she took every opportunity to put her work out into the world, and to be seen alongside it: non-juried art spaces, juried events, art fairs, live painting events, studio and gallery tours: "I made connections in the nearest city and with regional artist associations. I gradually grew to include events in many major Midwest cities and began reaching out to galleries. Eventually, I used these experiences and the relative success found at each one, to hone in on who my people really were." She is now more selective and intentional about where she chooses to put her work—to connect with the right audience.

She has also facilitated artist mastermind groups since 2019: small groups of artists who are dedicated to both continuing their own growth and helping others along their path. Megan enjoys the small group interactions, "where each person feels fully heard and worthy of contributing." She brings a lot of knowledge to these groups, with her own art practice, corporate experience, and gallery and curatorial experience: "But it's not about me teaching the group. I absolutely share my resources but I feel like my real contribution is in facilitating the group calls and online network in a way that elevates everyone's voice." ✳

"I often think about the way that life tends to be anchored by some basic structure and rules but needs a little unexpected chaos to blow through to stay interesting. I want my materials to act the same way."

TRANSFORMING THROUGH COLOUR AND LINE

For Megan, making art is a way of making sense. "I need to make art to 'complete' my experience of my life and the world we live in," she says. "I'm amazed that I have the ability to take these ideas and get them to translate onto a surface. I'm excited in a completely unique way when I see colour and line come together out of my own hands. Being able to bring spontaneity and intuition together with analysis and consideration to create a piece of art makes me incredibly proud. I think it's an absolute gift to be able to spend my days doing something that makes me both excited and proud of myself. We should all be able to do and feel that. I'm also passionate about seeing other people experience my work and feel big emotions as a result of it. Knowing that a painting I've created evokes joy, wonder, curiosity and happiness feels like a magic trick. And I also feel like everyone deserves to feel joy, wonder, curiosity and happiness—so I'm passionate about getting the work I make into the hands of people with whom it resonates."

Waupaca, Wis.
Aug. 2 1937

Regular meeting of the board of Directors of the
First National Bank, Waupaca, held on this date.
Meeting called to order by Pres. Benlick at 7.30
P. M. Directors present, Benlick, Nelson, Holden and
Stratton. Smith absent, out of the city.

Minutes of previous meeting were read and approved.

Loans and discounts nos. 4599 to 4713 read. Moved
by Holden, seconded by Stratton that loans as read
be approved. Carried.

After a general discussion of business and conditions,
meeting adjourned.

meganwoodardjohnson.com
@meganwoodardjohnsonart

EPHEMERA

"A major calling card in my work is vintage paper ephemera, collected from antique shops, thrift stores, estate sales and generous friends and family," says Megan. "I'm selective about what types of materials I use. I'm drawn most to paper that was once used to help a person." Her favourite ephemeral paper picks are educational items such as children's illustrated books, textbooks, reading primers, colouring books and penmanship workbooks. She also collects calendars, notebooks, shopping lists, maps, ledgers and product packaging—the stuff of everyday life. And then come commemorative paper things like greeting cards, letters and certificates. "I tend to prefer materials from the 1930s to the 1970s because the nostalgic qualities of items from these eras evoke memories attached to my grandparents, my parents and my own childhood. I have a strong emotional response to them."

Though the old papers may confer meaning, despite her graphic design training, she does not use them in a typographic way. "I do not use materials that are recognized for their content—I avoid legible words and recognizable pictures. I choose elements based more on the visual texture and interest they contribute, walking a fine line between materials that feel familiar and nostalgic, but do not contribute a literal or narrative element."

MUSGRAVE PENCIL COMPANY

THE *Heritage Collection*

ONE DOZEN OF OUR FAVORITE PENCILS

MADE IN U.S.A. · MUSGRAVE PENCIL CO · SHELBYVILLE, TENN · *Hermitage* 510 THIN RED

Choo-Choo 8500 MUSGRAVE PENCIL CO. INC. SHELBYVILLE, TENNESSEE MADE IN U.S.A.

MUSGRAVE PENCIL CO. GENUINE *Tennessee Red* CEDAR

MADE IN U.S.A. 500 MUSGRAVE PENCIL CO. SHELBYVILLE, TN 37160

MUSGRAVE PENCIL CO. INC. SHELBYVILLE, TENN. U.S.A. 909 CERES 2 BONDED LEAD

CUB MUSGRAVE PENCIL CO. INC. SHELBYVILLE, TN. 37160 - 3030T

MUSGRAVE PENCIL CO. SHELBYVILLE, TENN. *Unigraph* 1200 DRAWING

MADE IN U.S.A. 600 MUSGRAVE PENCIL CO., INC. NEWS

TEST SCORING 100 MUSGRAVE PENCIL CO. SHELBYVILLE TENN.

MY-PAL MUSGRAVE PENCIL CO. INC SHELBYVILLE, TENNESSEE - 2020

Harvest MUSGRAVE U S A 320 2

MUSGRAVE PENCIL CO. INC. SHELBYVILLE, TENN. BUGLE 1816 - NO 2

MUSGRAVE PENCIL COMPANY

As the great-grandson of James Raford Musgrave, who founded Musgrave Pencil Company in 1916, Harper Hulan treads the factory floor where many members of his family had gone before him. Harper is vice president of sales at the company. "When our great-grandfather founded the company, he somehow knew that Middle Tennessee had an abundant supply of Tennessee red cedar, a wood that had proven perfect for a pencil. So he cut it into slats and started selling the wood to German pencil makers." After a trip to Europe in 1919, James bartered for the machinery to make his pencils in Shelbyville, Tennessee, and the rest, as they say, is history.

The company does what it does and does it very well—making thousands of wood-cased pencils of all sizes (standard, hex, jumbo, bridge and carpenter) every day. They are still making pencils the same way they did a century ago. "Much of our machinery dates back to our founding. We have two machinists on staff who fix, maintain and even engineer parts for our equipment. They are very talented and always busy. We care about our community, and we care about the hardworking team members we employ. That's why we never sold our company or left Shelbyville."

Up until 2018, Musgrave Pencil Company operated as a white label manufacturer, making pencils branded by others. They didn't have much of a logo or web presence. The company was doing well, but the Musgrave brand suffered because of a lack of recognition and investment. "We knew that had to change," says Harper, "so we hired a small design firm from

"A pencil isn't what can change the world, it's the ideas and vision you have when holding it that will!"

nearby in Nashville, Studio Delger, and we started working with them to reflect our rich history in our branding." As the rebranding rolled out, smart new offerings appeared, like the bright yellow Heritage Collection, and a variety pack (and who, reading this book, doesn't love one of those?) containing a dozen interestingly named pencils: the 600 News, 1816 Bugle, 510 Hermitage, the 320 Harvest Professional, 100 Test Scoring, 909 Ceres, 500 TOT, 8500 Choo-Choo, 2020 My-Pal, 3030T Cub, 1200 Unigraph F and the Tennessee Red. And, for the carpenter who has everything, the fat and flat Sidekick Carpenter pencils appeared, aromatic of the red cedar wood from which they are made.

With billions of pencils produced since its founding, chances are you may have had a Musgrave-made pencil in your hands at some point. More recently, a new awareness of the brand has grown in the broader pencil community. Indeed, pencils have niche aficionados, and collectors rightly obsess about them. A pencil is such a simple, lovely thing. Its basic design has not changed for hundreds of years—though Musgrave has recently launched an entirely eco-friendly pencil, the Greenbelt, with a recyclable ferrule and a distinctive apple green latex-free eraser. Tapping into this pencil love has re-energized the company, says Harper: "This has been thrilling for us. We hope 100 years from now we're a household name and still employing wonderful people from Middle Tennessee and from within the Shelbyville community." His great-grandfather would be proud. ✻

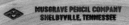

TENNESSEE RED

Musgrave's best-selling Tennessee Red pencils are made with eastern red cedar. "To understand why it's so special," explains Harper, "it's important to know about pencil manufacturing in the United States."

Due to the availability of eastern red cedar and a then-thriving number of pencil manufacturers, Shelbyville, Tennessee, earned the title the "Pencil City" in the 1950s. "But by the 1970s, pencil producers shifted away from eastern red cedar, opting for California incense cedar, which was more abundant and workable. As the story goes with US manufacturing, many businesses moved offshore in the 1980s, 1990s and beyond. Today Musgrave is the only remaining pencil manufacturing company in Shelbyville, and one of very few in the US. That means that most pencils today, no matter the manufacturer, are made with incense cedar or basswood and produced overseas. In late 2019, we decided to go back in time and make pencils from eastern red cedar. So we

launched the Tennessee Red—and later our Tennessee Round—that was a tribute to the original wood used by our founder. Musgrave Pencil Company is the only manufacturer in the world producing pencils using this kind of cedar."

MADE IN THE "Pencil City"

SHELBYVILLE, TENN.
SINCE 1916

HOW TO MAKE A PENCIL

A pencil starts out as wooden slats. Each individual slat goes through a machine called a groover that cuts grooves into the surface of the wood. This preps the wood for its graphite. Next comes the graphite core of the pencil. Each slat gets a thin layer of glue, and one by one, graphite cores are laid into the snug grooves that were cut into the slats. Once the cores are laid, the graphite is sandwiched together with another slat. This is the first step to a "wood-cased" pencil. The freshly glued slats are now clamped together and left overnight to dry, ensuring everything holds tightly together. As they are still slat "sandwiches," the next step is shaping the slats into pencils. Slats are laid into a cutting machine that divides each one evenly—shooting out raw pencils.

 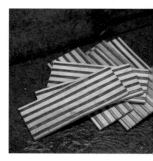

After cutting, the raw pencils are given between four and ten coats of paint. Once they are painted, they are printed. Some get hot foil lettering imprinted on the side; others will get digitally printed, a full foil wrap around the barrel or screen printed. Once the pencils are painted, printed or foil wrapped, they are "tipped," which involves placing a ferrule (a metal band that is crimped to hold the eraser) and an eraser on the end of the pencil, and clamping them in place. Some pencils are sharpened, using a belt sander to grind down the tip of the pencil into a fine point.

"A pencil is simple and utilitarian, and yet the starting point for creativity, education and human connection."

MYSTELE KIRKEENG

Making delicious portraits of women you might like to know, Mystele Kirkeeng tells stories with her brush that take us into both her world and the worlds of her women. Although she was not expecting art to play a leading role in her life, she is thankful it does: "I'm a rather ordinary human who was caught by surprise by the advent of art-making in my life. I started painting in answer to a prayer after finally starting to deal with years of depression. I think of painting as a concrete tether to sanity and shalom, a true Godsend."

Her paintings lean toward, as she puts it, a folky, naive storytelling expressionism. Her figures—for she mostly paints figures—fill the frame. Her mark-making style sees the paint living and alive on her canvases; the faces of the women, in particular, are made up of shapes and colours and textures that you might not expect will work together, but do. The women she paints represent the women in her life: "I mostly make figurative work of women who represent my African ethnicity with a Southern African American folk-art vibe. I'm beginning to venture into more work that will include more of my life's quotidian, although I'm sure figures will always play a prominent role in my work. I think at the core I want my work, no matter the subject matter, to be a subversive thread of wonder in the world and I am thrilled when someone else sees it for what it is."

From her studio in Crystal Lake, Illinois, she works in a tidy manner. Her studio—which she

"I am so thankful to be able to do this art thing. I never saw it coming, and now I hope I never see the day that I must let it go. It's a magical way to touch people and see myself more clearly. It's a gift."

affectionately calls The Imaginarium—is a spare bedroom in her family home and she has used every square inch: "There's not a lot of room to spread things all over. Keeping it on the tidy side also helps me keep my mind clear. I guess I'm a chaos wrangler all around. However, I know I would allow for more mess if I had more space." In those tidy drawers and pots, Mystele keeps favourite art supply materials to hand: "I enjoy working with matte acrylics, all sorts of pastels, pencils, charcoal, collage... oh gosh! There's *so* much to love. I enjoy having a variety of materials within reach because I want to be able to respond to my intuition with what seems like the right kind of texture, or mark, in the moment." Perhaps her favourite art supply is, she says, a good piece of junky under-paper from her main work area: "These papers catch the chaos of colour and marks and random collage from the workday. Some of my favourite paintings are abstracted from these cast-off papers."

Despite her organized studio space, Mystele makes her work in a freer way, giving meaning to the phrase "organized chaos": "I mostly work intuitively, without any plans, by means of abstraction, or pareidolia. On the rare occasions when I work with a plan or from a sketch, the feeling just isn't the same." She is inspired by the creative process itself, by where it leads: "Everything starts with some kind of chaos that I peer into, looking for a story to tell. One mark leads to another. Since I work intuitively, I never know what's coming. It is a glorious ride. I know there are subconscious things at play, pareidolia leading the way. But I never really know what's going on until the work is complete. It's fascinating. That keeps me coming back again and again." ✳

"We need each other's voices. We are not just our own. Painting provides me with one way to connect with and encourage people who I will probably never meet but am connected to nonetheless."

"I believe in the connectedness of the human race and all the beautiful stuff in the midst of the stresses and horrors we encounter. Creativity is a respite and a weapon that enhances, emphasizes, heightens our recognition of what it means to be alive, to flourish, to struggle, to hope when so much is stacked against us. I want to be part of that kind of culture shaping."

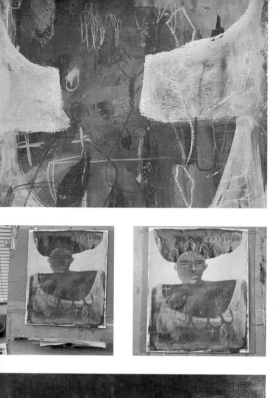

PAREIDOLIA

Pareidolia is seeing something meaningful—usually visual things, like faces in clouds—where nothing real actually exists. Until recently, it was a new word to Mystele: "I didn't know about the formal term 'pareidolia' until a couple years ago and only started using it as a descriptor recently." But she recognized the tendency in her own practice: "I used to call this process 'pulled art' because I felt like I was literally pulling the imagery out of the abstract ground/underpainting. Later on I began saying that I 'look in the paint to see what I see,' and that's truly the heart of it."

"All of us have a history of images and experiences that informs our creativity," she explains. "When you work intuitively with layers, what is familiar or interesting to you, those things you've known in your lifetime, show themselves. Often I only see a little bit of information that looks familiar, so I follow that." And as with any other painting approach, one mark leads to the next: "This abstraction is the impetus for what I do. I get so excited when the magic moment of awakening occurs, when I can feel something alive, something coming together out of the layers of marks and colour because I know that the adventure has begun."

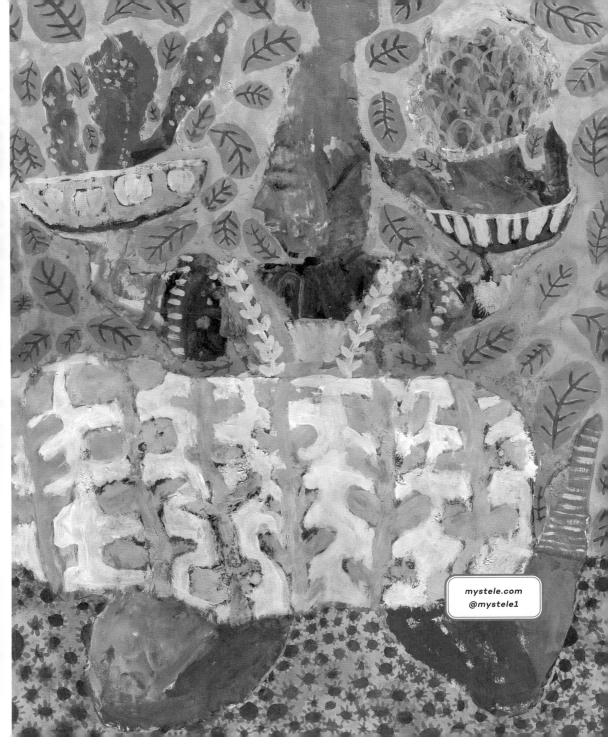

NATURAL EARTH PAINT

From a 100% solar-powered warehouse in Ashland, Oregon, the team at Natural Earth Paint make their range of non-toxic art supplies. The business is owned and run by Leah Fanning, an artist, mom and environmentalist. In 2009, with a one-woman exhibition coming up, Leah realized she would need to paint full time for a year to prepare for it. Pregnant with her first child, Leah was worried about the toxicity of her art supplies, so she ditched the lot and began looking for replacements. Finding nothing much, Leah took matters into her own hands, and just a few years later, in 2011, she founded Natural Earth Paint. A decade or so

"We recognize that we're always using earth's precious resources to create our products and so we do what we can to give back and to use the most eco-friendly packaging and ingredients available."

later, she now employs six to seven people and sells her natural earth pigments and organic ingredients to specialist art supply stores all over the world.

Whilst researching alternative art supplies, Leah had learned that almost all conventional children's art supplies that state they are "non-toxic" on the label actually include many toxic preservatives, carcinogens, petroleum-based dyes and heavy metals. She was determined to create high-quality face paint and art supplies that were truly non-toxic, natural and sustainably made. Diving down the rabbit hole of research on ancient paint-making recipes, she found out-of-print books on harvesting pigments, studied Renaissance techniques and conducted a long period of experimentation and testing. It took two years, hand-crafting paints from natural earth pigments that she collected in the Oregon woods, to get there.

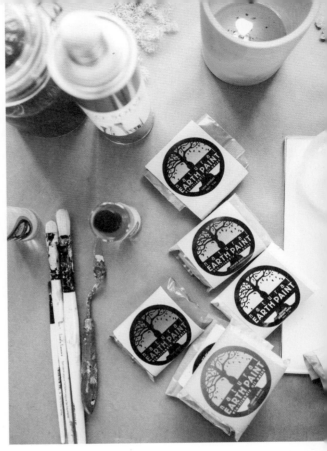

Natural Earth Paint launched with two kits: the Natural Earth Paint Kit (for children) and the Complete Eco-Friendly Oil Paint Kit. The children's paint kit contains six packets of powdered vegan paint to mix with water, six biodegradable mixing cups, a bamboo paintbrush and a booklet of nature-based activities. Making it was a labour of love for Leah: "As a mom and artist, I wanted my child's paintings to be beautiful and richly coloured and last a long time. So we created children's paint that is made with mostly pigment instead of a tiny percentage of pigment and mostly fillers and bulking agents, which is standard in conventional children's paints." The adult version, the Complete Eco-Friendly Oil Paint Kit, offers 10 earth and mineral pigment packets, refined walnut oil packaged in a recycled bottle, Eco-Solve paint thinner and a paint "recipe" book. Both kits are now bestsellers: "For the fine art products the focus is on purity, archival longevity and radiance of the paint, as well as the complete lack of toxins and synthetic or petroleum-based additives."

Their products include a mixture of ancient, traditional supplies and processes (paints and pigments) and newer scientific innovations like Natural Acrylic Medium, a recent innovation using plant-based resins and ingredients that can be mixed with natural pigments to make a truly non-toxic and plant/earth-based acrylic paint. They also sell Eco-Solve, a plant-based product made of soy oil with the fatty acids removed, and then processed in a way that gives it all the properties of conventional artist solvent but without the toxicity and fumes. Their Natural Varnish is a mixture of the two, as it is based on ancient recipes from the Renaissance but has been updated to eliminate solvents and toxic additives from the formulation.

"We strive to truly walk our talk and create quality products with integrity and to package them in sustainable or zero-waste packaging within a warehouse that creates no carbon emissions," Leah says.

In their solar-powered warehouse, they use very simple mixers and heating elements to maintain integrity in each small batch of products. "Our office also serves as a used plastic packaging drop-off site for local residents and businesses, which we then reuse to pack our outgoing shipments." Natural Earth Paint packaging is locally made from 100% post-consumer recycled boxes that are manufactured in a wind-powered facility. Their paint pouches are home compostable, the bottles are glass or metal, and the brushes and applicators are bamboo and vegan. Materials for their products are equally carefully sourced and tested. Earth and mineral pigments come primarily from France and Italy, and some areas of the US. The company spent several years testing pigments from around the world and found that the best colours and quality came from small, family-owned quarries that have been sustainably harvesting pigments for generations.

Leah's passion has paid off. Natural Earth Paint, a woman-owned and operated business, is thriving without compromising. "Many people don't realize that you can make almost every type of professional-quality art supply out there by just mixing natural pigment with different natural binders. By doing this you eliminate all of the toxins and fillers that detract from the quality of the art and poison our world." ✳

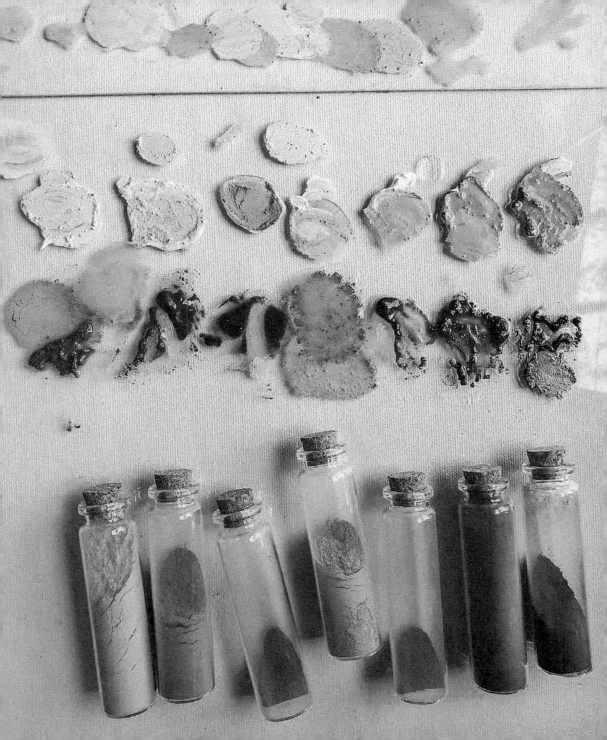

LEAH'S TIPS FOR A SUSTAINABLE ART PRACTICE

- Mix and store your own paints and art supplies.

- Rip up old T-shirts or clothes to use as paint rags.

- Mix paints on a glass palette instead of using disposable palettes.

- Use organic cotton (or hemp or linen) canvas to avoid high pesticide use in the cotton industry.

- Reuse wood panels or salvage wood to create stretcher bars.

- Get inspired by other eco-artists.

- "Reuse" your Eco-Solve: Just like conventional solvents, you can let dirty Eco-Solve settle for a few days, then pour out the clean solvent to reuse it, disposing the sediment.

- Investigate every art supply you use to find out about its ingredients.

- Paint over old paintings if you don't like them!

WHY USE NATURAL PAINTS?

Rather than unconsciously squeezing paint out of a plastic tube, a product that you have no idea what it is made of, or where it was made or by whom, you can instead purchase pigments and handcraft your own paint, forming a connection with pure, simple ingredients as you slowly mull your paints. As Leah says: "I like to think we're starting a 'slow art' movement, like the slow food movement. It's a return to the craft of art supplies—being present in each part of the art-making process."

There is a quality to natural paint that surpasses the manufactured product. Synthetic pigments are completely uniform in shape and size, so when mixed with oil and painted on a surface the light reflects off the surface and straight back out. Earth and mineral pigments, on the other hand, are natural and thus have irregular shapes with many varied surfaces and edges. When painted on a surface, light hits them and reflects off in many different directions, creating an intense chromaticity and luminosity that is unsurpassed.

Natural Earth's mineral pigment paints are also humidity resistant and lightfast. You could set a jar of their pigment in a sunny window sill for a hundred years and it will never fade: "If you think of the cave paintings, some that are at least 100,000 years old and still vibrant, they were painted with earth pigments and natural binders."

naturalearthpaint.com
@naturalearthpaint

NATURALLY SOURCED FINE ART SUPPLIES

ichelle Ryan became allergic to making art. "I was having negative reactions to my beloved art supplies," she describes. Michelle had developed allergies to a variety of chemicals, dyes, foods and scents, and she needed to make a change. Switching to an all-natural lifestyle, she sought an alternative to her store-bought, allergy-inducing art supplies. She discovered many stories of people from all walks of life going through the same thing. "It relaxed my anxiety about the environmental sensitivities I had been gifted."

"I started foraging materials—rocks, shells, flowers, trees and leaves—to make paints, inks, charcoal, crayons, pastels, art papers, mixed media and clay.

"I encourage artists of all mediums to practise sustainability in any way they can. Choosing art supplies for a sustainable future—it's time for change, to take a chance and reset back to our ancestors' ways."

Grinding them down with a mortar and pestle revealed beautiful colours. It's a process that gives you a deeper understanding and appreciation for the natural world around us." Her watercolour paintings, postcard art and greeting cards include the delightful line: "painted with 100% natural pigments from the earth."

Much of her work looks to local Celtic traditions for inspiration: "paying homage to four of the main languages based in Cape Breton (Mi'kmaq, Gaelic, French and English), mixed with Celtic knots and provincial tartans." She was born and raised in Nova Scotia and lives in Port Hastings, where she feels a deep connection with the beautiful wilderness, wildlife, native land and seascapes: "I have always been drawn to nature, rivers, woods and wildlife; the Maritime provinces are my favourite place to be!"

Michelle hopes that Naturally Sourced Fine Art Supplies, her new business, will become known for supplying safe, all-natural alternatives for art supplies. Nothing gets a maker closer to their work than making their own supplies. Michelle wants to communicate the positive process of making paint the natural way: "The raw materials I use in the making of my art supplies are all-natural pigments sustainably harvested from quarries around the world. This gives a wide variety of bold, natural archival colours, superior to toxic commercial brands. I have sourced my raw materials from various Canadian suppliers, which gives me the best range of pigments for mixing unique custom colour palettes." She makes all her watercolours with a glass slab and muller.

There is growing concern about the toxic aspect of many things in our lives. Artists work up close and personal with their supplies, so sourcing safer options makes a lot of sense—for both the artist and the planet. Michelle urges artists to find out if their art supplies are non-toxic. The list goes on and on, she notes, of symptoms associated with using products with toxins in them: "What you may think is a harmless hobby may very well be much more harmful than you think. I believe once you make the switch, your artistic creative thoughts will change with it. They did for me."

Developing allergies changed Michelle's life, "in a way I would have never imagined it would," she adds. "I had no idea how this experience would ground me. I became passionate about sharing my experience with my peers—and to continue to study the old way and walk barefoot in the garden." ❊

- Repurpose, reuse and recycle whatever you can, wherever you can.

- Reduce purchases on mass-produced products and buy quality products from local artisans.

- Stay away from disposable and single-use products.

- Preserve local small business barter systems.

- Be eco-conscious in how you shop.

- Mix your paints and use natural dyes.

"Mix your own paints from pigments; dye some paper with beets or blueberries and add some leaves and ferns for patterns. The possibilities are endless; once you start looking at your natural surroundings for this purpose your thinking process will be on a whole new wavelength. It is a wonderful feeling knowing exactly where your ingredients are coming from and that they are completely non-toxic!"

ALTERNATIVES

Michelle has eliminated all plastics, and reuses and recycles everything else. All items and supplies are 100% cotton, reusable or natural, plastic free and environmentally friendly. Experimenting with an alternative for plastic paint pans, Michelle has developed some satisfying all-natural clay paint pots to hold her colours. They will be one of the products available to buy as the business grows. She also collects various shells to include in her packages. She powers her shop with 100% green energy and makes monthly donations to offset her carbon footprint: "I truly enjoy the process of making natural art supplies to use for my artwork. It gives me a connection to the earth, and the environment around me, in my creative process. It is more than just going to the store and purchasing mass-produced inks and paints. It's an intentional practice specifically gathering raw materials and supplies such as clay, leaves and flowers, as well as recycling all my paper waste into new art projects."

naturallysourced.ca
@naturallysourcedfineartsupply

Nicholson's
PEERLESS
WATER COLORS
...the self-blending colors

COMPLETE EDITION

TRAVEL PALETTE

Nicholson's
PEERLESS
Transparent Watercolors

- color guide & travel palette -

Nicholson's Peerless Transparent Watercolors

Olive Green

Myrtle Green

Mahogany
Brown

Nile-us

PEERLESS TRANSPARENT WATERCOLORS

During the early days of photography, Nicholson's Peerless Transparent Watercolors made dry sheets of watercolour that photographers could use to colourize and tint their black-and-white photographs. Founded in 1885 by Chaz Nicholson, the company has had a few owners since, including current owners Dalton Scolman and his wife, Cassie, based in Fort Atkinson, Wisconsin, who bought the company in 2019. "My wife, Cassie, and I are the fifth owners of the company and are so proud and excited to take on the stewardship of such a storied and historical company!" says Dalton.

"The majority of our techniques and recipes are the exact same as our founder, Chaz, created over a century ago," he explains. The DryColor watercolour sheets are made with a concentrated wash of pigment on the back of a sheet of fabric-infused card stock. On the other side is a sample wash—an example of what the final colour will be like. The artist uses a moistened brush (Dalton can testify that using lake water and snow works as well, if need be) to activate the colour, ready for painting. The sheets dry quickly, making them portable and perfect for travelling and storing.

Ease of use is important to the company, as they are on a mission to demystify art and creativity. Dalton explains: "So many artists, including myself, have such a hard time with their inner critic. And now, thanks to social media the number of 'outer critics' artists have to deal with has gone up exponentially. Because of this many artists are caught in the trap of

"We try and design our paints and our palettes to be as easy to use as possible. With our paints, all you need is a wet brush and some paper to start painting."

buying art supplies and then being too terrified to even open them up and try them out. We want to make creativity and experimentation part of the artistic process again. We want artists to know it's okay to have fun while they paint. You get the inspiration to paint and our paints are already waiting for you." These are truly paint-and-go art supplies.

Nicholson's Peerless Transparent Watercolors is also building its eco-credentials in a sustainable way. All of their raw materials are non-toxic, environmentally friendly and ethically and sustainably sourced. Since Dalton and Cassie bought the company they have also moved towards using either fully recycled material or biodegradable material for packaging: "We haven't reached 100% sustainability in that area but we will very soon." Over a century of business is a testament to the efficacy of a product. And it is lovely that people care enough about the heritage of art supplies to spend their lives keeping lovely old products alive and kicking: "I'm just so incredibly grateful that this community of artists supports our little family-run business. Because of the people who regularly buy and use our paint I am able to keep my family fed and keep this 130-year-old tradition alive. I love doing this and I love seeing artists create works of art they love with our paint." ✳

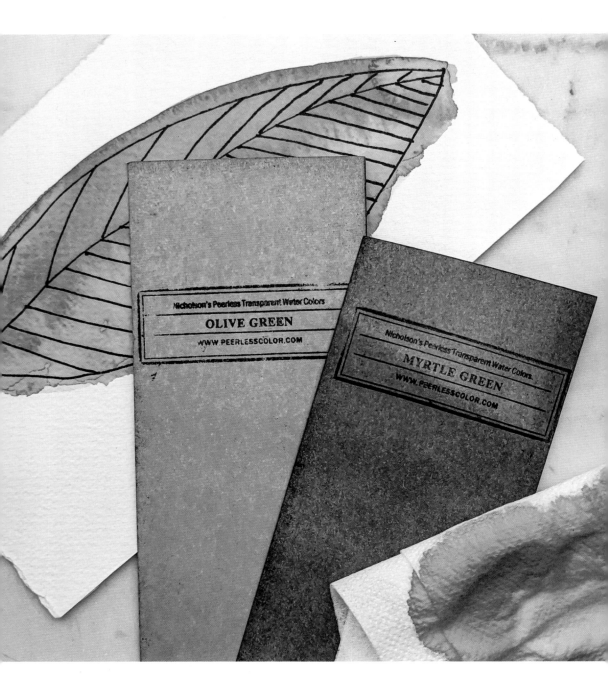

Nicholson's Peerless Transparent Water Colors

OLIVE GREEN

WWW.PEERLESSCOLOR.COM

Nicholson's Peerless Transparent Water Colors.

MYRTLE GREEN

WWW.PEERLESSCOLOR.COM

"I think a good step in creating a sustainable art practice is supporting companies that go out of their way to maintain sustainable practices—especially when it is not their cheapest option. With time, I hope and believe that the sustainable options for businesses will start to compete financially with their less sustainable counterparts. Supporting small paper makers is another great place to start. Something that I like to do is capture rainwater to use as my water source to activate my paint."

THE COMPLETE EDITION

"We use vintage and original drying racks along with industrial, human-powered paper cutters to create our products," describes Dalton of the making of Peerless watercolours. The majority of their techniques and recipes have been the same for over 130 years. "It's a long and arduous process." Each concentrated colour is the result of layer upon layer of paint applied by hand.

The oldest and most popular product at Nicholson's Peerless Transparent Watercolors is called the *Complete Edition*, a booklet filled with 15 transparent, handmade watercolour paints, all stapled into a yolk-yellow paper booklet so as to be easily found in your backpack. The booklet contains old English colour descriptions and painting tips as they were originally printed in 1902. The 15 colours have not changed over time: Brilliant Yellow, Deep Yellow, Orange Yellow, Ripe Peach, Geranium Pink, Japonica Scarlet, Royal Crimson, Mahogany Brown, Sepia Brown, Light Green, Dark Green, Deep Blue, Sky Blue, Wistaria Violet and Pearl Gray.

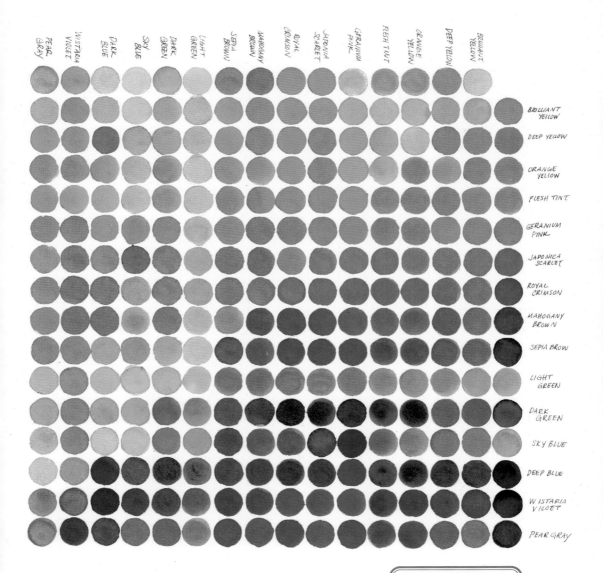

PEARL GRAY · WISTARIA VIOLET · DARK BLUE · SKY BLUE · DARK GREEN · LIGHT GREEN · SEPIA BROWN · MAHOGANY BROWN · ROYAL CRIMSON · JAPONICA SCARLET · GERANIUM PINK · FLESH TINT · ORANGE YELLOW · DEEP YELLOW · BRILLIANT YELLOW

BRILLIANT YELLOW
DEEP YELLOW
ORANGE YELLOW
FLESH TINT
GERANIUM PINK
JAPONICA SCARLET
ROYAL CRIMSON
MAHOGANY BROWN
SEPIA BROW
LIGHT GREEN
DARK GREEN
SKY BLUE
DEEP BLUE
WISTARIA VIOLET
PEAR GRAY

peerlesscolorlabs.com
@peerlesswatercolors

PEG AND AWL

We all need something practical and beautiful in which to keep and carry our beloved art supplies. This is where Peg and Awl step in as makers of plein air painting kits, sketchbooks, bags, art and arty things. Owners Margaux and Walter Kent's story started with a little happenstance.

On her first trip to Europe many years ago, Margaux purchased a handmade journal that later fell apart. Then, her bag—with the crumbling journal in it—was stolen. This unfortunate event compelled her to make a better journal on her own. "I credit the thief with starting me on this extraordinary journey. It became my mission to find a book bindery and when I did I was transformed." Using 100-year-old scrap leather that she removed from chairs at an upholstery shop, she made her first book. "I bound a book (using my thighs as a press) in a glasshouse in Ireland, in a rainstorm." The beautiful journal was much admired, and along came requests to make more. She started a company called Black Spot Books and met Walter soon after. "We merged all our doings—woodworking, bookbinding, jewellery and photography—and started Peg and Awl."

The business began in their home in West Chester, Pennsylvania. "We started in our home, just me, Walter and our son, Søren, who by age three started sanding and tying tags," Margaux recalls fondly. When they could no longer keep up with the demand, the couple's parents jumped in to help. "Eventually, we hired our hodgepodge team from various

"We love the look and depth of marks of time—caused by unknown hands—all surfaces imbued with the genuineness of daily human pursuits."

backgrounds—including gardeners, musicians and filmmakers—people with the desire to learn new skills and use their hands to make objects that they could feel good about."

"As we shared our knowledge, our skills evolved—not just in making and art, but in all of the things small businesses require, including attention to detail and problem solving. With each new employee (and the team has grown to 16), we learned a little more about how to work together as a team." Eleven years since that beginning, Margaux and Walter (plus sons Søren and Silas) have created a culture that attracts others who are also excited to come and be "part of the magic."

Although Peg and Awl began without a plan—just an affection for making things they felt were missing in the world—they have flourished and now have a much extended product range that includes jewellery, workspace objects and furniture. The notebooks continue, some covers lined with unique vintage textiles such as 1930s feed sacks or ginghams from the fifties. The bag range comprises everything an artist could need, from artist rolls to backpacks, including the Sendak Artist Roll and Scout Plein Air Box and other carryalls. "First and most importantly, we make useful objects that will endure, with the hope that they will be used for a long time and repaired when needed," says Margaux. "Second, we seek sustainable and local materials whenever possible. And we use as much of the materials as we can, leaving little waste." They use minimal packaging and safe, natural finishes on the products, and spend a lot of time sourcing the best materials they can find. Four times a year they put together "Of a Kind" collections, incorporating found, antique and vintage materials: "This harks back to the origins of Peg and Awl, and it allows us to continue to seek and be inspired by materials of the past."

Both Margaux's and Walter's earliest memories are of making objects and art, and "perpetually scribbling." They have been fortunate enough to turn their

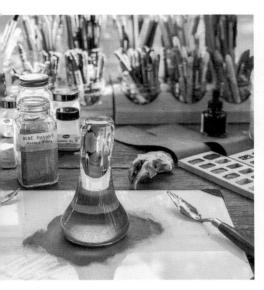

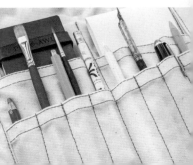

passion for making things not only into a business and how they make a living, but also into something they can share with their boys. Work and life are very much intertwined at Peg and Awl. This is set to continue, as they are presently converting a barn near their home (The Five Acre Wood) into a woodshop, with areas for bookbinding, paint making, drawing, painting and workshops.

The Peg and Awl children are homeschooled and the family ethos is of learning, travelling and making art, together. "Our curiosity is endless. Exploration fuels our learning and growth as a family and as a business. We get to remain curious because this is where the magic is—in the adventuring, a kind of pause from work. These pauses lead to discoveries and pivots— whether resulting in new products or new processes, once again, we start out for ourselves and then share with everyone." ✳

QUEST FOR MATERIAL

"Our work is inspired by necessity and usefulness," says Margaux. Keeping that same attitude when it comes to sourcing their raw materials, Peg and Awl uses reclaimed materials—and they will go to great lengths to find them.

For leather goods, after an informative trip to a 500-year-old tannery in the United Kingdom, Margaux and Walter were inspired by their new understanding of sustainable and responsible leather and sought something similar state-side. "We found Wickett and Craig in Pennsylvania. Their leather is made from a slow, natural and eco-friendly process of tanning raw hides with natural, biodegradable extracts derived entirely from vegetable sources. This durable leather breaks in and gathers a gorgeous patina, bearing the marks of the users' (and makers') adventures—the very thing we've always celebrated!"

For reclaimed wood, their pursuit led them to the Alan McIlvain Company, a supplier of sustainable hardwoods for the last two centuries. "We now make most of our products out of FSC-certified hardwood, a certification that ensures that trees come from responsibly managed forests that provide environmental, social and economic benefits."

Vintage textiles and materials are featured in their much-anticipated Of a Kind collections of pretty zip pouches and one-of-a-kind objects that quickly sell out.

"We started our business making things with old materials that would otherwise have been added to landfills. We used old-growth wood from homes and barns torn down locally, leather from flea markets, old textiles found in abandoned houses— all objects that came to us."

"Our materials are important to us," Margaux states, "so we put a lot of time into finding the right ones. Often, the adventures themselves become just as valuable."

"Eleven years since our beginning, our team still does everything it takes to run a business— from imagining to prototyping, designing to manufacturing, creating systems and plans, shipping, marketing and customer service! We started this business so we could spend our days doing what we love, and as we've grown, we have created a culture that attracts others who are also excited to come to our workshop and be part of the magic."

"Whether we have five minutes or five hours, our blank pages await. Art has become a daily practice for us. In real life, or on social media, the objects, the tools and the work inspire conversation and community."

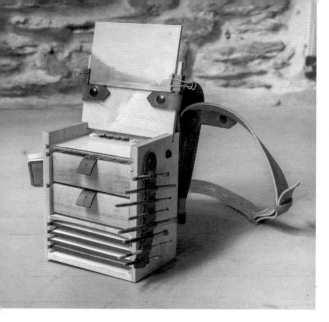

THE SCOUT
EARNS ITS BADGE

The Scout Plein Air Box was one of the first artist-specific products that Peg and Awl designed from the ground up. It is the crème de la crème of pochade boxes (from the French word *poche*—pocket—and the proper name for an outdoor painting box) and it started with an adventure, as many of their products have: "Walter headed to Italy for a plein air painting retreat—a kind of painting that was new to him. The only one without a box, he immediately began to envision his ideal setup."

After a year of trial and error, they launched the Scout in 2020 to much excitement from customers. Walter's process began with sketches, which he turned into working test versions. He used and adjusted these prototypes until he was pleased with the design, use and ease of the box. Most of the materials, including the wood and leather, are things they already used. But particular parts, like the glass palette and pre-primed canvases, came from collaborations with local companies.

Walter thought of everything for the Scout: there is an exterior and an interior pocket, slots for drying canvases and two binder clips to hold them afterwards, an adjustable shoulder strap, two drawers (magnetic), a wooden easel, snap-on jars, a snap-on brush holder (holding eight brushes) and eight empty paint tubes—all wrapped in FSC-certified walnut or maple from southeastern USA.

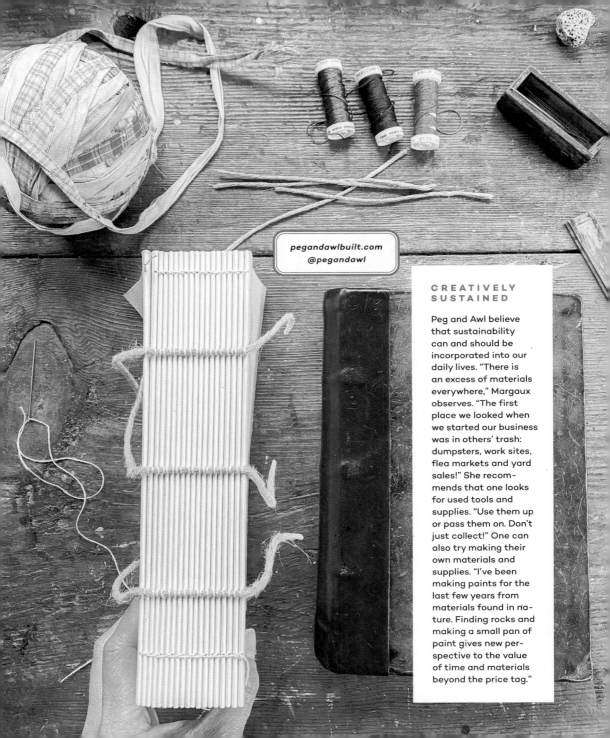

pegandawlbuilt.com
@pegandawl

CREATIVELY SUSTAINED

Peg and Awl believe that sustainability can and should be incorporated into our daily lives. "There is an excess of materials everywhere," Margaux observes. "The first place we looked when we started our business was in others' trash: dumpsters, work sites, flea markets and yard sales!" She recommends that one looks for used tools and supplies. "Use them up or pass them on. Don't just collect!" One can also try making their own materials and supplies. "I've been making paints for the last few years from materials found in nature. Finding rocks and making a small pan of paint gives new perspective to the value of time and materials beyond the price tag."

THE PRINT FROG

I n a book such as this you might expect to encounter some rather niche art supplies. And who better (and more motivated) to invent them than artists trying to solve a problem? In 2013, printmaker and inventor of the Print Frog glass baren, Matt Bagley, found himself in need of a new tool to help him with his own printing process: "I had a project where the blocks were too warped to run through the press. Printing was aggravating my repetitive strain injuries that had resulting from printing with wooden spoons, cheap plastic and traditional barens. I dreaded printing this edition. An efficient baren was desperately needed. A friend suggested glass as a material."

Matt worked with a local glassblower to make his first glass baren, a hand tool for printing relief blocks without a press. The trial glass barens surpassed his expectations. Rather than make just one, the glassblower produced about 40, in different sizes and shapes. Matt shared these prototypes with fellow printmakers and they quickly became a desired tool: "We started receiving emails asking if we had any more. We quickly realized that other printmakers had the same frustration with hand-printing tools. I refined my design and coined the name Print Frog." The name comes from when Matt was setting up his printmaking studio, Iron Frog Press, in 2010: his parents had given him a small frog trinket made of iron, "and I couldn't resist naming my shop after it."

By 2014, Print Frogs, the first production barens made from glass, were available to buy. It turned out glass was the ideal material because it is heavy enough that the artist who is printing doesn't need

"The Print Frog is the most efficient, easy to use, comfortable, durable and versatile glass baren available to printmakers."

PHOTOS BY SHARON NEEL–BAGLEY
PRINTMAKER, BEN MUÑOZ
PRINTMAKER, KATE WINNOWS

to exert extra pressure (potentially causing problems like Matt's repetitive strain injuries). It is also a low-friction material, so there is less rucking of the paper. Glass is also easy to clean and is durable. In 2016, Iron Frog Press introduced the Pro Print Frog, which is, Matt says, best for big prints and big editions, glass plate printing and encaustic monoprinting. They then named the original baren the Studio Print Frog; it works best for small to medium relief blocks such as linoleum, wood and MDF. Matt also recommends it for printing on fabric and says it works great for printing damaged blocks, collagraph and chine-collé. In 2019, they developed two smaller models: the Froglette Print Frog is designed for very small wood engravings with delicate details and substrates, and the baby of the range, the Tadpole Print Frog, is for using with tiny blocks and rubber stamps.

Matt and his wife, Sharon Neel-Bagley, now have a small business making their amphibian baren family. Along with their two assistants they still run the Iron Frog Press, a "backwoods fine art press" printmaking studio where artists can produce prints. They also have a mobile printmaking workshop called Print-Shop a Go-Go, with which they take print out into the community, spreading the printmaking joy. ❊

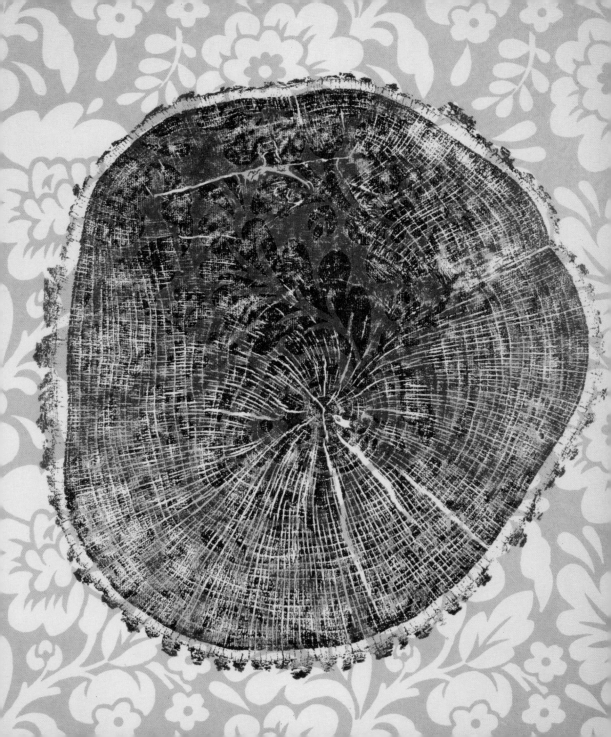

ACCESSIBILITY

Print Frog makes printmaking more accessible to artists, since you don't need a press to set up a production printshop. Matt suggests that the glass baren is an accessible tool that can be used by self-taught artists, and that elderly and differently abled people can return to printmaking. It can also be part of an "off-grid print shop," he says.

VERSATILITY EQUALS CREATIVITY

All types of relief blocks—wood, linoleum, rubber, plastic, metal, clay, glass, plaster, etc.—can be successfully printed with a glass baren on a variety of substrates, from delicate papers to thicker sheets, cloth and even leather. "You can print blocks efficiently that cannot be run through a press," explains Matt. "It's a great companion for a traditional press and also allows for a variety of non-relief print techniques." He lists bleed edge litho, chine-collé and monoprints of all types as other expressions made easier with a Print Frog.

"Chill marks, a smooth rippled texture found on the bottom of the Print Frog glass baren, result from the glassblowing process. After extensive testing, we found that these chill marks enhance the performance of the Print Frog baren. The large knob handle fits comfortably in hand for all-day printing. The radius edge on the bottom is for focused printing for delicate and challenging details."

GLASS MASTERS

The master glass blowers with whom the Iron Frog Press work are in the North Texas area. They use two types of glass to make the Print Frog range: borosilicate and soft glass. The Pro, Froglette and Tadpole barens are made with borosilicate glass, a superior material often used to fabricate cookware and scientific equipment. The Studio, the original baren, is made from recycled soft glass. Both kinds of glass offer the heavy weight, low friction and durability that make them an ideal material for a baren. Borosilicate glass is a superior material because of its strength, low friction, heat tolerance and ability to form precise shapes and surfaces. Soft recycled glass was the original Print Frog material and is much quicker to produce. As Matt explains, "These Print Frogs tend to have a more organic shape and feel. Our soft glass Print Frogs are made from recycled glass and our glassblower has lots of colours available."

ROBEN-MARIE SMITH

Our creativity is often rooted in childhood experiences. Growing up, Roben-Marie Smith moved from place to place; her father was in the military. "My journey to a creative life started at a young age," explains Roben-Marie. "To cope with the difficulty of fitting in and making friends, the perfect outlet was to spend time creating something—anything, really. And so it went, moving and adjusting and making new friends." She had found a constant: "I discovered there was something magical about creating with my hands."

"I dabbled in many forms of art and craft during my life, but when I discovered art journaling and mixed media, a fire was ignited in me to learn as much as I could about combining artful expression with words. I had finally found a form of expression that was a great fit for me. I began developing my style and never looked back."

She remembers her mother sewing matching outfits for her and her sister when they were young. Her mother also taught her how to sew, a skill that factors into Roben-Marie's present-day art practice. These days, settled in Port Orange, Florida, Roben-Marie can often be found at her sewing machine, which has become her favourite creative tool. "It's so much more fun than a paint brush or a stencil. As a child, I made stuffed animals and learned to manipulate fabric. When I discovered mixed media as an art form, I had the lightbulb moment of testing out sewing on paper. I love how sewing adds texture to my art, and leaving the treads hanging in my work is an added bonus of fun and whimsy."

"As a creative person, mixed-media is a way for me to express myself. I thrive in the studio and feel more confident when I am bringing ideas to life through painting and collage."

Her mixed-media works, collages and handmade art journals contain layers of tissue-like transparent colours, vintage papers, wax crayon and pastels marks, stitches and shapes. They are abstract, yet not, as you try to pull a subject out of what you are looking at. "The process of creating something beautiful with the art supplies I love is a joy that is hard to describe. I especially enjoy paper collage from assorted painted papers I have made myself. There is something therapeutic and calming when I sit and cut bits of paper and arrange them into a 'new story' that I can share and use to inspire others."

By consciously mapping her own artistic development, Roben-Marie has moved from a conservative, less-is-more approach, to something much more bold and wild: "There was a turning point in my evolution as an artist that was very unexpected and it happened when I realized that I had been reticent to use colour, as I felt that was the domain of 'real artists.' My fears and presuppositions were erased and my confidence grew. I became a different artist after that, embracing both colour and my talent in a new way. It changed everything."

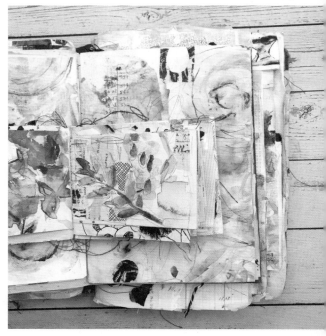

Roben-Marie has been a working artist since 2004. "I'm self-taught, so I believe that anyone can cultivate their creative spark. As an artist, instructor and woman of faith, my mission is to serve others and help them get the most out of their art as a hobby, or as a business." Roben-Marie is an art teacher and a tech champion. "As my confidence grew as an artist, this led to years of travelling and teaching at art retreats, where I discovered a real love of teaching." This led to the creation of online art courses, which enable her to combine her love of teaching with her love of technology. She founded Maker's Tech U, an online membership community for creatives, helping them with the technology and online side of their creative businesses.

In her journey toward finding peace when calling herself a real artist, Roben-Marie had to look deeper into her own past and her practice. As she discovered, art was her way of bringing beauty into the world and where she could be herself: "I journal because it is so personal. I am not content to simply document with just the written word. I need to express myself with colour and texture and images. My art really reflects my personality because I put so much of myself into what I create. Art is where I can let go, where I don't have to worry about rules." ✽

"Art is meant to be shared—to encourage and inspire others. There is a reciprocal relationship that strengthens both the artist and the audience, which makes facing down those fears worthwhile. It can be intimidating at first to put yourself out there but I have found it very rewarding. I encourage every person with a desire for art in any form to start, just jump in, no delays. Be bold and just *do*."

INSPIRATION ABOUNDS

It sounds cliché, but truly inspiration is everywhere. My favourites are magazines, catalogues and a spirit of curiosity. I stay focused and motivated by my love of experimentation. I am always open to adding new mediums, products and techniques to my work and love to find a unique spin on the tried and true. I love discovering a new skill set that I did not know I possessed. Trusting that what I am is "enough" and pushing through the doubt and dry spells that plague every artist is what keeps me going, season after season. I am increasingly aware that refilling with rest and quiet is one of the most motivating gifts you can give yourself.

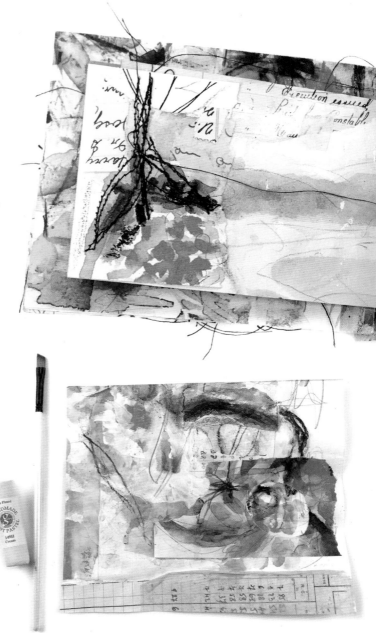

MIX IT UP

"Seriously," says Roben-Marie, "what's not to love about art supplies? Who needs candy stores when we have Dick Blick!" (Dick Blick Art Materials is an art supply chain with more than 65 retail locations in the United States. It was founded in 1911 and now has over 8,000 products sold under its brand name.)

Roben-Marie is drawn to a variety of mixed materials. "I guess you could say I am multi-passionate," she explains. "Over the years, I have tried a lot of mediums but I always come back to my love of paper. I enjoy combining watercolours, soft pastels, pencils and crayons in a messy and organic way. I am drawn to inexpensive sketchbook paper mostly because it wrinkles and takes the mediums I use in a way that makes me happy. It's mysterious and tactile."

She likes to combine non-traditional materials in order to get unexpected combinations: "I especially love the look of soft pastels mixed with water. The chalky watercolour effect is beautiful." Her signature material is her paper, which she creates—not from scratch but through painting and layering with unique marks and painted shapes. And sometimes bits of stitching are added for texture.

robenmarie.com
@robenmarie

SARAH GOLDEN

I n 2015, when her two girls were 18 months old, Sarah Golden devised a plan. "My goal was to be doing art full time by the time they started first grade." This gave her a few years of working odd hours in the studio without the pressure of making a full-time income. "I was able to hone my craft, my vision, and figure out how to run an art business. Once preschool started I was working full time."

Sarah is a fine artist and surface pattern designer. Her modern paintings and collages are bold and beautiful, with colour and shape writ large. "I create abstract paintings, a lot of times painting on a large unstretched canvas tacked up on the wall and then cutting a piece down to get the composition to my liking. I like having the hardness of the wall as resistance while I'm painting." Her paintings are rather like the

"My motivations are always to grow as an artist, explore and keep expressing my artistic voice, always aiming for more deep work in my studio practice. I want people to live with my art, on their walls, on their clothes, in their cupboards, with the cards they send. For me, that's the joy and freedom of being a fine artist and surface pattern designer."

pieces of old wallpapers and storied paint layers you might see on a wall in an abandoned house.

Cup of coffee in hand, Sarah starts her creative day with an overview and inventory. Taking a tally of what size canvases she has, what she needs to order, how she will present the work, the frames required, the timeline for release, how many pieces there will be in the collection, whether prints or photography are required and so on. "I'm cerebral in the planning stage," she explains. "I love spreadsheets, and getting the numbers down. Then when I start painting, I work intuitively. I like to work on about six to ten paintings at once, creating a history with layers and layers." She likes "going in" with a pencil or big graphite stick, "scribbling and scratching" around. Sometimes she paints a whole block of colour, covering up half her canvas but leaving the brushstrokes from previous layers showing: "I paint on canvas and wood panels, using acrylics, graphite and acrylic mediums. I love that a painting can have infinite layers to it; it creates a visual history. Acrylics are awesome for layering,

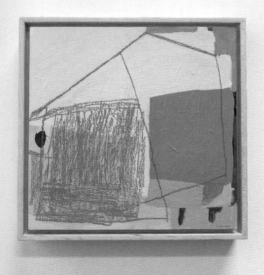

since the drying time is quick. I like to work on multiple pieces at once so I keep my workflow when I'm in it and it keeps me from overworking one painting." With her typically smaller collage works, she uses vintage papers with lots of mark making in graphite and ink, with painted papers and cardboard to build up texture and dimension: "I really enjoy the intuitive nature of piecing the compositions, the repetitive work in it, the cutting and glueing. I lose myself in it."

Taking a break from painting to turn to digital work is something Sarah relishes. "When I'm creating patterns for licensing, it's taking that work, scanning it, turning it into repeats or print quality. It's a lot of computer work! I also work digitally in Procreate. I take a day a week and most evenings to do that. I sit on the couch and watch television while I draw. Honestly, I made some of my best work that way. Being slightly distracted helps me not overthink and overwork the artwork. I love bouncing back and forth from painting to digital work."

Her systematic approach combined with an excellent work ethic has allowed Sarah to craft a career that is both creatively fulfilling and full of possibility. "It's my job and it's also my obsession. I truly feel incapable of working for someone else, in an office or more traditional job, wearing professional clothes— please no. I wanted to build a creative business that would support my family and myself." She now has the freedom to create artwork, to put it out there, to allow it to become something else, to take on different meanings with someone else: "And that is just so satisfying." ✷

A DREAM SPACE

Sarah's studio space has gradually increased over the years. It began as a room shared with her husband, but soon she took over the whole room as her own. By 2019, she had rented a studio outside of her Sacramento, California, home in an art building in the city's downtown. "That studio was 180 square feet, but I also had my home studio which was my design studio and I'd work on small paintings. The other studio was solely for painting. It was awesome to have that dedicated space, but ultimately I realized working from home was ideal for me and my family. So I moved out of that studio after only six months and we decided to build my dream space in the backyard and to go big, a space I wouldn't grow out of, space to hire help, host events and evolve my large-scale work."

Working with an architect and builder team, her dream studio was built in 2020 in the family's backyard. With 16 windows, 5 skylights and 15-foot ceilings, the natural light is incredible. "It's just a few steps from the house and I love the convenience of it. There's a 200-square-foot loft upstairs: that's my office and design studio. Downstairs is where I paint and have my print studio and shipping area. I have a main painting wall, which is 20 feet wide and 12 feet of plain wall. This allows me to make giant paintings and have a lot of canvases going at once. Having a space like this to walk into and make work in has been a game changer for me."

Sarah is grateful for this space that sparks her imagination and supports her creative endeavours. "Planning projects on my giant work wall, having the ability to paint larger than I ever have... Walking in here in the morning, with all this natural light and space, is breathtaking every single time."

COLOUR!

"Colour sets my brain on fire," Sarah says about attractive and energizing juxtapositions of colours. "This is how I feel when I see two colours that sit next to each other in a certain way." Colour palettes are gathered from buildings, photographs and even through repurposing her own work. "I have a file on my phone where I keep colour inspiration photos and screenshots." She purposely does not take such inspiration from other people's artwork. "I get it elsewhere and siphon it into my work. My artwork could be inspired by the colour of a semi truck and some vintage tiles in a bathroom."

She works on her colour a lot, thinking about how a piece feels when she walks in the room: "I want to create work that brings good energy to a space and to people. At the same time, enjoying the process myself is extremely important. I like to work in different mediums, explore and get creative with how I create work, whether it is an original piece of art that someone hangs on their wall, or a pattern on fabric, or housewares that people bring into their homes and enjoy daily."

sarahgolden.org
@sarahgoldenart

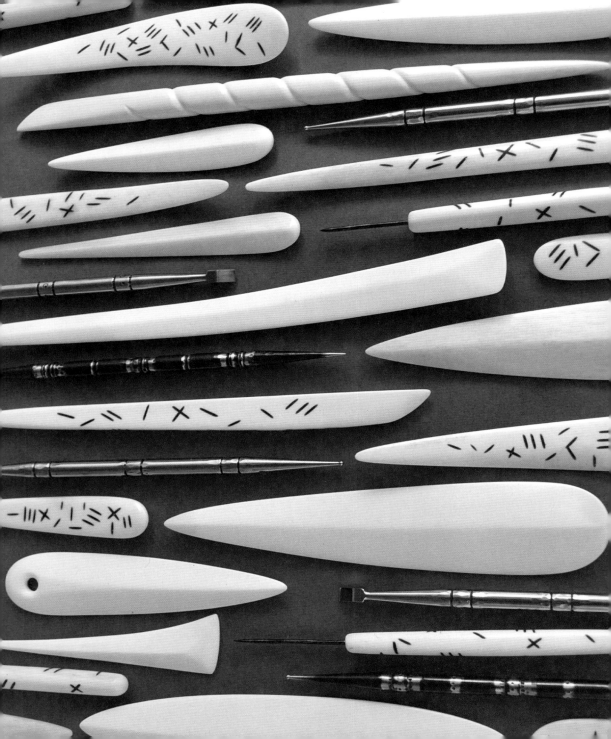

SHANNA LEINO

Shanna Leino brings thought and care to the making of artist tools. "I am passionate about beautiful, quality tools," she says. "I design and produce the tools and accessories I want to use myself. Sometimes I also refurbish and repurpose vintage and antique tools, often adding my own decorative elements to them."

As an artist working in multiple media, Shanna's interest in making things wanders far and wide: "I like learning new skills and experimenting with materials, then combining what I've learned with what I know in simple ways that expand my work. I seek out rabbit holes to fall down."

Like many artists who also supply a product, her business grew from things she made for herself. Whilst studying at the University of Iowa's Center for the Book (in Iowa City, Iowa), Shanna found her community. "When I found my true love—making books—I needed certain tools to carry out the work I wished to make. The skills I learned in printmaking, wood and metal shop, and jewellery gave me the ability to make my own tools. Then, as I travelled around using the tools I made while teaching workshops in bookbinding, others asked to have similar tools for themselves. And, fortunately for me, a business was born."

She makes various things: a double-ended steel awl (with a tiny ball on one end, stylus on the other, used by bookbinders, crafters and printmakers for hole poking, scribing and scoring), bone folders (a very simple and satisfying bookbinding tool to fold and crease paper) of all shapes and sizes made from

"I am passionate about beautiful quality tools. I design and produce the tools and accessories I want to use myself."

ROBERT HENSLEIGH AND SHANNA LEINO

elk bone, small micro-chisels, a stainless-steel Kelm folder (named in honour of bookbinder Daniel Kelm) and her heavily engineered Mountain Fold denim apron, "specifically designed to accommodate a woman's curves."

Because she suffers from "an unquenchable need to try out new ideas," Shanna brings in new items from time to time, in small batches: anything from a magnetic felt and leather pin cushion; to leather polka dot paperweights, spoons and scoops, jewellery, pouches and parchment-wrapped stones; to her Loopy Awl— hand-carved from locally harvested wood such as walnut and lilac. It is an eclectic product selection, everything existing somewhere between function and fantasy. "I love the process of making a prototype and figuring out the first iterations of an idea," she says.

Shanna has refined her products by user-testing them herself: "As a maker I find it necessary and satisfying to use a tool that performs its task well and

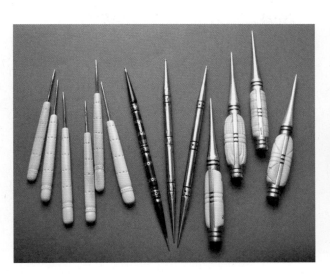

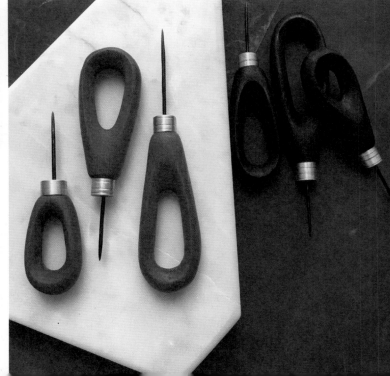

that is also aesthetically pleasing, whether it is for my studio or kitchen or garden. Being surrounded by useful beauty bolsters my spirit, gives me confidence and dignity in my work, and often sparks inspiration out of the blue." Shanna likes learning new skills and experimenting with materials, something that she has plenty of reason to pursue while developing new products: "Take a flame, for instance. It can be used to harden, soften and liquify metal; join metals together; adhere glass to metal; and colour metals and wood. A person can have a lot of fun with a plumber's torch. I like seeing how much I can push the equipment and materials I have on hand."

Shanna works at her home in rural Frankfort, Michigan. Her studio at her house is a large, separate space with lots of light and, she says, is often in a state of perpetual mayhem as she works through batches of various tools. "There is music playing always, and art by friends and heroes hang on the walls to inspire me and remind me of how fortunate I am to be a part of such an extensive, passionate, fun and supportive community while I work away in solitude. Within arm's reach I have my most indispensable and often used equipment: a flexible shaft rotary tool, a dust

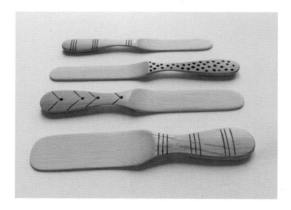

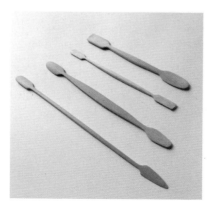

CONSIDERED IMPACT

Incorporating sustainability into one's art practice can be creatively rewarding as well as good for the environment. "Using natural materials enhances my work and is no encumbrance, since there is incomparable beauty to be found in the grain of wood, the drape of natural fabrics, the creamy tones in elk bone, the density of wool felt," says Shanna. "I delight in being able to compost the leftovers of my work, or better yet, use the wood scraps to spark up the sauna. It is my hope that what I make will endure and serve those who use what I make for as long as they need them, and then be handed on to the next person."

SHANNA'S PRACTICAL IDEAS

- Work with sustainable and natural materials.

- To the best of your ability, own less of better quality for longer.

- Be an educated buyer.

- Lighten your load, pass along duplicate and un-used tools and materials to those just beginning or to local arts organiza-tions and schools.

- Find ways to re-envision things that can't be recycled.

- Share what you've learned with others to help make it easier for them to make these choices.

- Vote every chance you get.

- "Take up spoon carving," she recommends. "Preferably in a chair out in nature. You'll spend countless, focused, contented, unplugged hours contemplating the character of wood and the ways of humans. The mind will drift and ideas will pop up. I'm banking on solutions for our greatest challenges coming from time spent in this way."

collector, a 100-pound anvil and hammers, assorted files of all shapes and sizes, a jeweller's saw, pliers, mounds of in-process tools that I'm working on, a cup of coffee."

Down the driveway from the house is the barn, which holds her big mess-making equipment—a bandsaw, belt sanders, and grinding and buffing wheels—though she enjoys working outside in the open sky when she can.

Of her manufacturing process, Shanna admits to taking a divergent approach, one that can be both exciting and frustrating. She works with other industries, such as machinists, CNC manufacturing and cut-and-sew manufacturing, to bring her ideas to life. "I love having a glimpse into the vast world of ever-evolving technology," she says. "It invigorates me to see how modern capabilities can combine beautifully with traditional materials and approaches." ❋

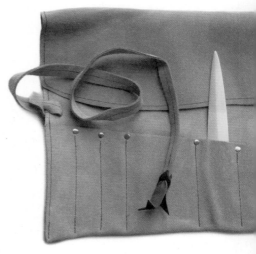

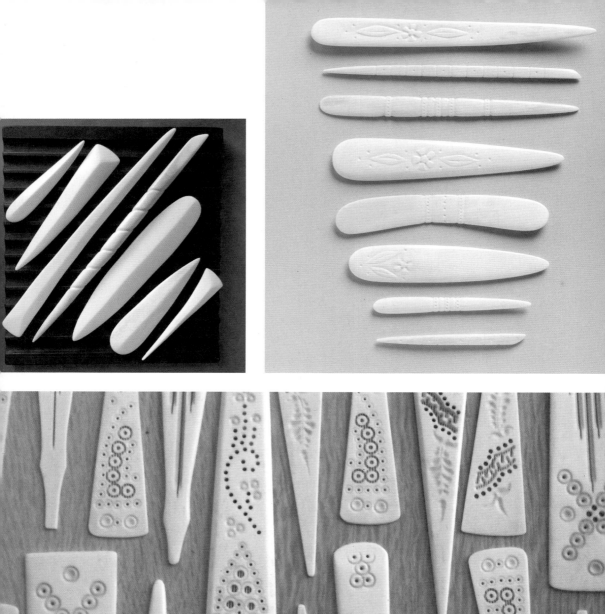
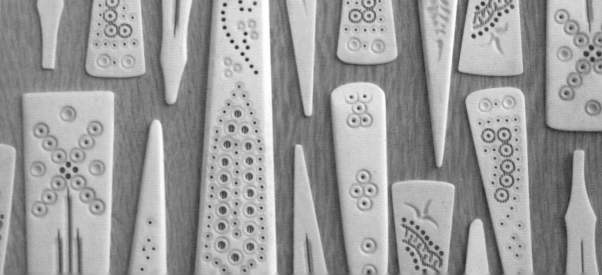

RECYCLED BONES

The most unusual and labour-intensive material Shanna uses in her work is elk bone. She was introduced to the material by the bookbinder and tool maker Jim Croft, who taught her how to make her first bone folder: "The process is dirty and smelly. I receive a box of cleaned elk leg bones in the mail from out West. The bones come via hunters—the elk meat is harvested by game processors and the bones would be thrown in the trash if it weren't for those specialty businesses that clean and sell bones, pelts and so on to craftspeople and taxidermists."

She then drags her bandsaw out into the yard and hooks up dust collection: "I put on all my safety gear (P100 respirator, ear protection, safety glasses) and cut the leg bone into slabs, taking care to get the most usable pieces from each bone. From there I move on to a belt sander to do coarse material removal and establish the shape the tool will become." Then after a shower and a change into fresh clothes, she moves inside to her studio, to work with hand files to refine the shape and surface of the bone folder: "Next I decide what decorative method I will use: Hand engraving? Adding lines with a jeweller's saw? Shaping with a file? Inscribing with a rotary tool? A combination of approaches?" The final cleanup of the bone folder is carried out with progressively finer files, then sandpaper, then it gets a buffing on a felt wheel.

shannaleino.com
@shannaleinohandbuilt

SHELLEY DAVIES

Collage maker, painter and editorial artist Shelley Davies takes using art supplies to the next level—she uses art supplies in their entirety, packaging and all. She has used vintage paint boxes, ink bottles, sellotape tins, half-used oil pastels in their box, old paintbrushes, erasers, scissors and strings, rulers and even tiny cracker-surprise-sized paint palettes, amongst other things, in her kaleidoscopic work. She plays with her unusual materials in a serious way, colour-matching everything perfectly, building each image of disparate found pieces into a coherent graphic whole.

Shelley was always headed for a life of creativity, one way or another. "I was that kid who was always making stuff," she says. "I knew I was an artist at the age of five, when I saw, hanging in a large and very silent contemporary art gallery, Jim Dine's huge painting with a bathroom sink attached to a black, paint-splattered canvas. Whatever that mysterious thing on the wall was, I wanted to be a part of it!" It has been a rather winding road, however: "After a few too many art schools, I tried to sink myself into the world of large, colour field painting, a life-long love of mine. I changed tack when I realized the world already had one Ellsworth Kelly." She spent the next 10 years working in the animation and film world. And there were some major life changes: "Motherhood and the creation of two fine young men (my best work to date!), with moves to Holland and England for 12 years, and then back to Canada to begin an illustration career rounded out my happy, zigzag creative path."

"I love a treasure hunt, and searching for a colour, an object or a piece of type to fit a project is the best fun, whether it's on distant travels, at a local flea market, or in my studio. The spontaneity of the find is often so unexpected and invigorating to the process that it brings a freshness to what's being made, and usually sparks even more ideas."

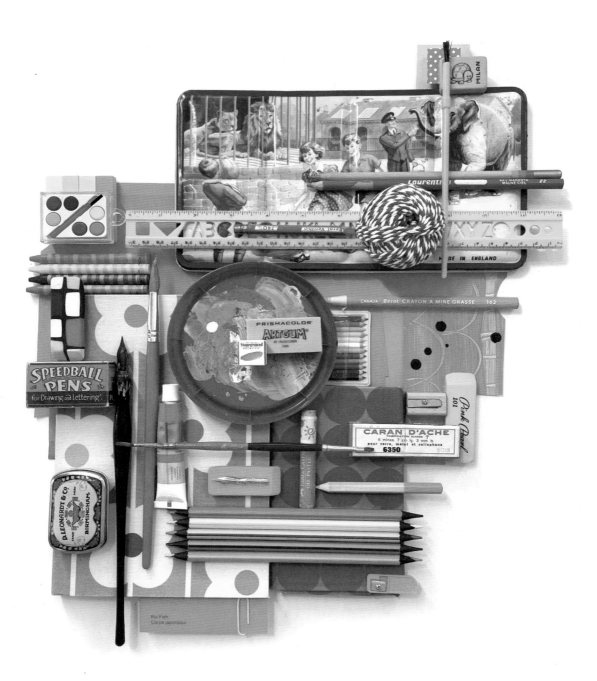

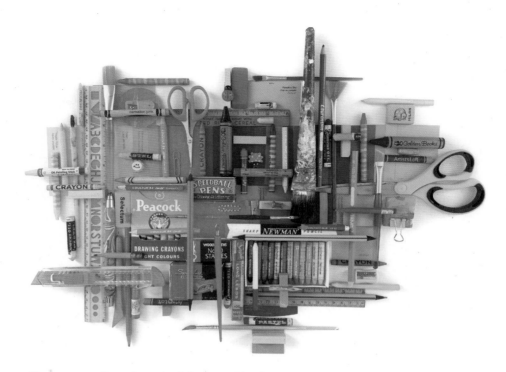

She came to collage almost by default, working for magazines and newspapers. She was forever botching up illustrations and needed to find a way to fix the mess before the deadline: "Presto, I discovered that collage could accommodate all the flaws and mistakes and turn them into attributes! With that eureka moment, a creative gear started to turn, slowly, and I began to find my creative feet." Shelley mainly produces individual collaged artworks and assemblages, and she likes to draw all kinds of paper flotsam into both aspects of her work: "I know what I'm attracted to (typography, bold graphics, beautifully aged ephemera—things with their history etched on their surfaces, and vibrant colour), and do my very best to incorporate as much of this stuff into my art as is possible. Sometimes I throw all of it at what I'm doing, and then have the happy task of editing it down to a distilled version of the jumble sale that it starts as. It's fair to say that I'm quite happy to embrace a bit of chaos in my work process. I love to see what rises to the top of the mess. The distillation is the fun bit. The art of subtraction!"

"There is more than enough stuff on this planet to interact with, to have a creative relationship with, to make art with. It's not necessarily the materials themselves that are valuable, but the spirit we invest them with, which is that magical intersection of humans and art-making."

"As I love to make things from found objects
that are already in the world, I don't feel I'm adding to
the ever-growing pile of detritus here already.
Perhaps I'm just rearranging a tiny corner of our world."

Shelley embraces play throughout her process. She likes to make playful art, she likes to play whilst making it, and she likes to have playfulness come through to the viewer: "I figure the world always needs more play, both for children and for adults. We lose that sense of play as we get older, and then we forget how to do it altogether if that muscle isn't flexed—and I believe that can translate to all areas of life. We find it much harder to entertain ideas when we're rigid, so play, in all aspects of our lives, seems essential to me for creative living, thinking and relating to each other." Embracing play as part of her process means embracing unexpected outcomes in her work, too: "I've never been one who strives for perfection. That was never my goal, and the fun factor wasn't nearly high enough for me to aim in that direction. Life always seems to intervene, spilling, splashing and undermining any attempt at perfection and finesse."

With experience comes confidence in one's practice and where it fits in with the wider picture. "As I mature, both as an artist and a human," says Shelley, "I do my best to embrace the uncertainty, the mistake, the unknown outcome of what I'm attempting to create." ✳

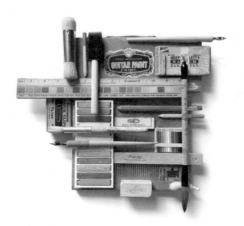

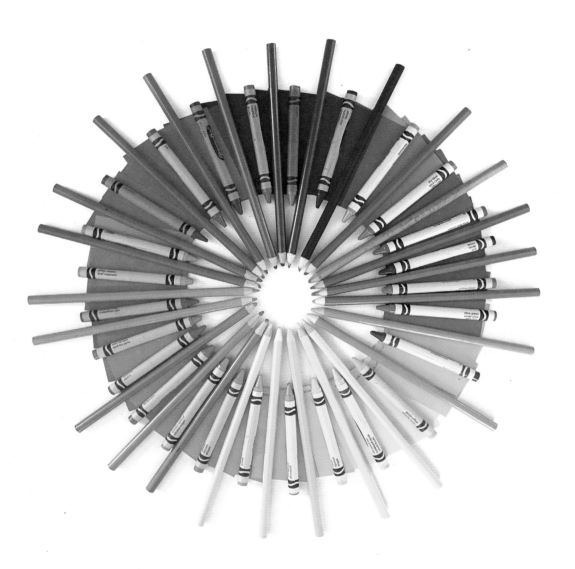

"I'm particularly passionate about colour. I'll cross many lanes of heavy traffic to get to a colour that's calling to me."

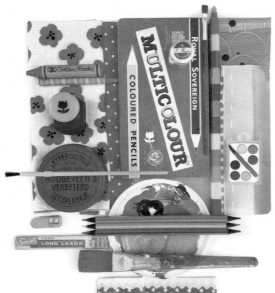

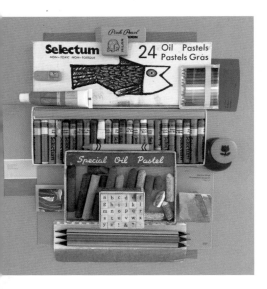

A close companion to play is curiosity. Artists are always asking, what if? "I think my passion comes from a deep curiosity about what will come next if something is put in motion," agrees Shelley. "If I put this colour, shape, object or letter here, what will beckon to it? What will make it sing? And when the singing starts, so does the fun. Energy starts to flow, and I want to find out what happens next. And it can be as simple as putting two colours side by side. Electricity is created! There's an energy that thrums through colour, a vibration, a life force, that excites me on so many fronts. It breaks language barriers, transcends age gaps and so effortlessly brightens visual life."

Curiosity is Shelley's motivation. It always leads her to something wonderful, something just around the corner. She nourishes curiosity via a "seemingly endless" love of books: "With a rather large home library, my cross-pollination of ideas is sometimes hard to trace back to its source. Perhaps it's the bouillabaisse of this curiosity that creates its own juxtapositions in me, but that seems to be an excellent place to begin."

Technology has given us instant access to inspiration, constantly on tap, but as delightful as this can be, Shelley feels it can become overwhelming very quickly. Instead, she has learned to tune out the distractions: "When a spark of inspiration hits (which can be so tiny and evanescent sometimes) I'm much better at putting down the book, turning off the computer and getting down to work than I ever was. I'm able to acknowledge now, as I get older, that the thing I'm searching for is that thing only I can create, the thing yet to be created. And the only way to find it is to get to work. That excitement, of what is to come, inspires me to keep looking, keep messing around, keep committing to work/play, as it always leads me somewhere."

shelleysdavies.com
@shelleysdavies

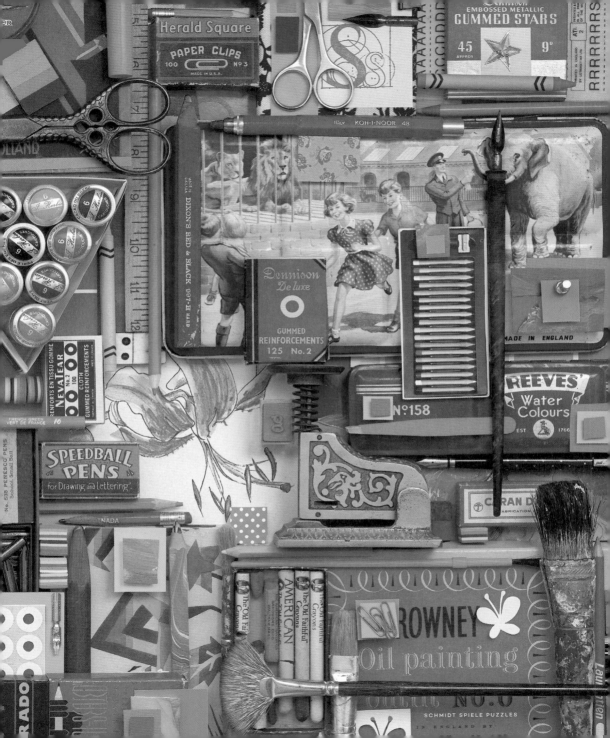

STENCILGIRL PRODUCTS

Stencilling as a mark-making technique can be traced back over 35,000 years, when prehistoric peoples placed their hands against cave walls and blew pigment around them, leaving a silhouette of where their hand once was. Today, we typically use stencils in the opposite way: masking off areas where we don't want a design and using the holes in the stencil as the intended graphic motif. Beyond applications in printmaking, labelling, signage, graffiti and home décor, stencils can be used as an art-making accessory.

StencilGirl founder and owner Mary Beth Shaw, a mixed-media artist, set up her art stencil business in 2010 in response to workshop students wanting to purchase her stencil designs. Growing from just six inaugural designs, StencilGirl now offers over 2,000 to choose from, representing the designs of over 100 internationally known artists.

The company began in the basement of Mary Beth's home in Ballwin, Missouri. The company of seven has only recently moved to a 1,000-square-foot building across the parking lot from Mary Beth's studio. "Our facility has a couple of areas. There is a laser room that allows us to corral the Mylar bits and pieces that previously cluttered our home. Storage, shipping and packaging dominate the rest of the space."

Initial stencil designs are converted into a laser-ready file, such as an EPS file. The stencils are cut from Mylar, a specialist heat-resistant plastic sheet, sourced in the USA. At seven mil thick (a mil is one-thousandth of an inch), the stencils are durable but thin. New designs are tested for structural

"We adore people who are passionate about creativity!"

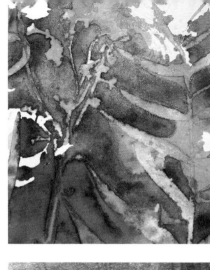

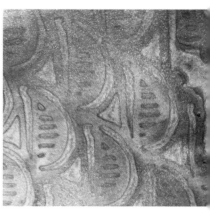

integrity: the design must be strong and long lasting. Stencil "islands" are a design that is *inside* a hole. Think of a stencil of the capital letter A, and how the triangular counter of the letter must be attached to the stencil with a "bridge"—the narrow piece of material that connects it to the overall stencil.

The artist then has an opportunity to test the stencil and determine if it meets their own standards for design and works for its intended process. As an artist herself, looking after their contributing artists is important to Mary Beth. The company bears all costs of helping each artist develop stencils. "Many of our artists do not have graphic design training but we work with them to make the best stencils possible with respect to quality and artistic design. Our licence program allows the artist to maintain ownership of their art and we pay royalties each quarter based on the number of stencils sold." Their business model focuses on education: "We seldom advertise. Instead, we give stencils to teachers who help us spread the word by teaching students of all ages how to incorporate stencils into their artwork."

To avoid waste, StencilGirl stencils sold directly to consumers are not packaged. Most customers appreciate the lack of packaging, but the company has also developed a product they call StencilGut, a way of using leftover pieces of Mylar: "This is waste produced during manufacturing that we save and organize into categories that are usable to our clientele," says Mary Beth. "I have developed a couple of art techniques using the StencilGuts. I don't clean my stencils and they can develop a layer of paint after a certain period of time. I use these 'thick' stencils along with the 'guts' in a variety of different ways, from including them as a collage element in my art, to glueing them onto a collagraph plate for printmaking." They also limit production to four sizes of stencils, which minimizes their footprint in a number of ways, including storage and packaging.

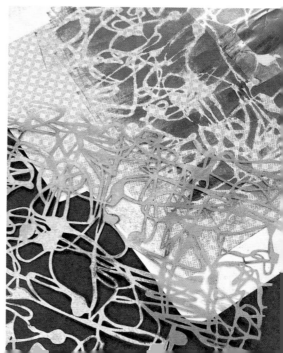

The StencilGirl community is supported with the StencilClub, started in 2013. Subscribers receive exclusive stencils along with a project and have a private community where they share and show each other what they have made. As Mary Beth says: "We view part of our role as discovering every way a stencil might be used." Stencils are incredibly versatile tools: "An artist can use the full stencil or just a part of the stencil. They can flip them over to create mirror effects and cut them apart to create an entirely new tool. They can be used with paint, ink, pastels, texture pastes and encaustic paint on a wide variety of surfaces, including paper, wood, walls, fabric, glass and ceramic." StencilGirl sells stencils of nearly everything, from letters, words and numbers, to circles of every persuasion, to bestsellers like puddles, faces in the crowd and a "love collage." These are tools that might help with artist's block or simply give you a starting point for some creative fun, messing about with your art supplies. ✽

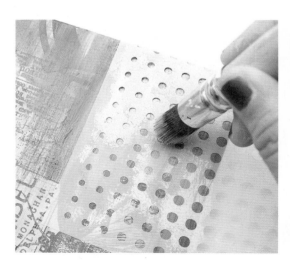

ARTISTS AND COLLABORATORS

Mary Beth finds her StencilGirl artist collaborators in a few ways: some artists contact her directly, some she discovers on social media networks. Others she meets teaching at art retreats—and indeed, artists who are teachers are ideal: "There is a learning curve using stencils, so an artist who plans to teach using the stencils is important. We want artists who intend to actually use the stencils themselves in their own work. Bookmakers, collage artists and those interested in making painted papers and fabrics are perfect."

Carolyn Dube is one of their most prolific artists: "I met her at an art retreat, then she took a class with me, and subsequently started working behind the scenes for us. As her experience level grew, she became interested in teaching mixed media to adults and designed a few stencils. From that initial moment, she exploded in a very good way. She specializes in gel plate printing and is well respected."

Rather than give her artists a specific brief, Mary Beth wants her artists to design the stencils of their dreams: "the kind of design that people would wonder how it has even been transformed into a stencil." They help artists to adapt designs so that they work as a stencil. As for the advantage of working with StencilGirl: "They gain a ton of exposure by working with our company, through our promotions and social media networks. In addition, they earn passive income from our royalty program. They gain confidence in their promotional abilities through building multiple income streams."

stencilgirlproducts.com
@stencilgirl_products

STEPH BEZZANO

Sometimes adversity proves to be a life changer. Steph Bezzano handmade her first sheet of paper at university in 2018 whilst studying for a fine art degree. Her practice sat within the expanded field of drawing, exploring the interrelationship between paper and line: "Paper's passivity as a traditionally flat drawing surface was challenged as I manipulated handmade paper to become something physical in space. I made a two-metre-tall freestanding handmade paper sculpture, and a long handmade paper line that wrapped round and enveloped the architecture of the gallery." However, two years on after graduation, Steph felt a bit lost. "After graduating, I struggled to navigate my way creatively and work without the luxury of the technical equipment I'd been lucky enough to use at university."

During a pandemic lockdown in the UK, and with the university facilities inaccessible, Steph revisited the craft she had loved, but with a new at-home approach. "I began to teach myself the process in the garden using materials that I had to hand. As my understanding and appreciation of the process grew, and as artists contacted me wanting to work on my paper and display my pots in their homes, my small experiment during lockdown turned into my full-time job, and I couldn't be more grateful."

She runs her business by herself, "with a little behind-the-scenes help from my family," making environmentally conscious, experimental, small-batch handmade paper and paper pots in Leicestershire, England. It is a very hands-on craft: "Papermaking is

"I love paper because it is tangible: the weight of a handmade paper sheet in your hands, the sound it makes when you shake it, the limitless possibilities of a blank sheet of paper to an artist and the physical connection I have with each sheet made by my two hands."

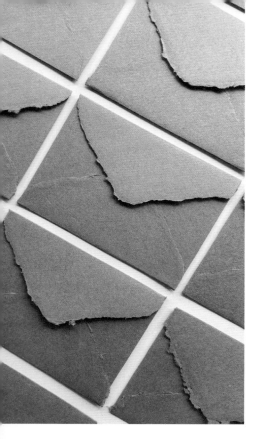

a physical process, as each sheet is produced by my hands, with the final sheets evidencing elements of their making—the weight determined by how much pulp used, bubbles and lines determined by technique. The materiality of the paper is at the forefront of my making. The tactile and weighty sheet that is produced is unique and evidences a conversation between maker and product, and each represents an individual moment in time."

Steph champions the use of domestic tools in her process. Her kitchen blender sees more pulp than pepper; every single one of her handmade paper sheets and paper pots are made entirely from waste paper donated by businesses, schools and households in her local area. Where possible, her equipment is secondhand and readily available: "The beauty of this process is that anyone has access to the tools needed to make paper—a simple blender, a mould and deckle made from two old photo frames and a press made by clamping two pieces of wood together."

SLATE

GREY

DENIM

CORNFLOWER

FERN

BRICK

PEARL

TOFFEE

CREAM

WHITE

Her papers come in a delicious range of ice cream colours, refined and developed through months of experimentation. They are, Steph says, "a reflection of all the colours I love in paper form." Each of her colour recipes are devised through intuition: "My process is kind of 'a bit of this and a bit of that' until I settle on what feels right, and generally I am able to achieve what feels right the first time. As my papermaking process uses waste materials, the composition of the shredding I receive always varies, which in turn varies the outcome of each finished sheet, despite sticking exactly to the recipe—sheets with more ink will make a darker pulp, for example." This adds an extra element of excitement to her day, as she never really knows what colour the finished paper will be until everything is dry.

Both her paper and her pots have a distinctive look and feel, the marks of difference that come from hand-making paper with recycled materials that have had a past life. The element of chance, which is an integral part of Steph's process, produces great paper: "The tactile nature of handmade paper is an enhanced experience compared to working on paper. The sheets are weighty and totally individual, with deckled edges and a unique surface, and are a tangible outcome of a physical process." The natural and unique elements in her papers have created interest from painters looking to enhance their own practice. They use her papers to add an extra dimension to their own work. ❋

A SHORT GUIDE TO (SUSTAINABLE) PAPERMAKING

When making her handmade paper sheets, Steph shreds waste paper and soaks it in water overnight to soften it. The wet shredding is then blended with water to form a pulp, and colour is added if desired. Steph uses pigments that are safe, non-toxic and environmentally friendly, or she might combine coloured waste papers to create one-off runs of paper. This pulp is then added to a vat of water, and a mould and deckle is used to pull a sheet. The mould and deckle frame is submerged into the vat and lifted out swiftly, with pulp from the vat getting trapped on the mesh on the mould. The new handmade paper sheet is then left on a flat surface to drain. This drained sheet is then transferred (couched) onto some fabric, pressed to remove all the excess water and dried to reveal a brand-new handmade paper sheet. Currently, each of Steph's handmade paper sheets and paper pots is made inside her humble and pulp-splattered garage, on a large wooden table made from reclaimed, secondhand wood.

potsandpaperbysteph.com
@potsandpaperbysteph

Quinacridone Red Gold
Mayan Red
Quinacridone Magenta
Manganese Violet
Indanthrone Blue
Vivianite
Roman Black
Hooker's Green

STONEGROUND PAINT CO.

Stoneground Paint Company is a handmade watercolour company in Regina, Saskatchewan, Canada. "We are a family business, with my dad and mom, Eric and Julie Rowe, at the helm," says Jenny Rowe, creative director and principal paint-maker. Jenny grew up watching her father, a self-taught artist, paint. Her father has over 40 years of painting experience, and around five years ago, when expressing his dismay with factory-made watercolour, Eric decided to craft his own paint. "We have grown from one paint-maker at a small counter (me!) to 15 paint-makers in a workshop crafting handmade watercolour with pigments sourced from all over the world," says Jenny.

Eric's watercolour background greatly informed the direction of the company. It is very much a "by artists, for artists" company, with an artist at the helm and a variety of artists employed full time, making paint. Jenny has a degree in art history and a graduate degree in history. Combining research and history with watercolour and paint making feeds her soul daily. At its heart, Stoneground is a family concern: "My partner, Russel, joined the business a few years ago to help with the increased workload involved with the online and wholesale side of things, and our 12-year-old daughter, Rowan, had a pencil in her hand the day she was born, and now makes the occasional batch of paint for her mother."

"Historically, artists had a deeper understanding of their art supplies, often sourcing their pigments and making their own paints," explains Jenny. "Their binders were made by hand, and pigments sought out

"Stoneground paint is colour in its purest form: single pigment and binder. Give anyone the rainbow and tell them to go play—it's amazing what happens!"

PHOTOS BY JENNY ROWE, BRITTANY PERRY AND JUSTIN CHOMYN

based on their properties, effects or rarity. Their art-work was only as good as the supplies they created for themselves. We are passionate about re-establishing the lost connection between artists and their supplies."

Stoneground Paint Company sells an inspiring selection of watercolours in categories such as Earth, Metallic, Mineral and Pearlescent. The packaging features a honeybee, in homage to honey's important role in the manufacturing of their watercolours. The attention to detail is impressive, and each colour is listed on their website with potential uses and other colours it might play nicely with. Their pared-back product offer allows the pigment (and therefore the colour) to shine through, literally: "Our traditional approach to paint making without the use of fillers, extenders or preservatives results in bright, clear colours with beautiful luminosity and depth. The use of single pigments leaves colour mixing in the hand of the artist, helping to avoid muddy colours." Before you have bought any paint, your brush will be twitching for some Autumn Fox, Bone Black or Smoky Plum.

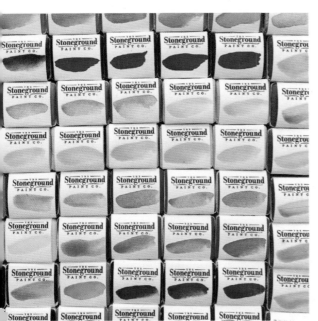

Quinacridone Magenta

Aureolin

Autumn Fox

Hansa Y

India Yellow

Gambog

Giant Orange

PO 34

Diarylide Yellow

Marigold Orange

Tiger Lily

Autumn Fox

You can buy each paint individually, but they also put together palettes that come in lovely small silver tins with a hand-painted colour swatch inside. "Each pigment is carefully considered and tested before production begins," explains Jenny. Her father's familiarity with paint drives the creation of the palettes they build for their customers. The palettes are named after the seasons, or are selections of, say, their pearlescent paints. Others are a little more romantic, such as the Night Garden palette or the Sea to Sky palette.

An artist from the 15th century would understand what they are doing, and yet slow making with traditional but modernized recipes has proved a success for Stoneground Paint Company. "It's incredibly satisfying to connect centuries worth of artistic tradition and skills to a modern era of artists," says Jenny. "I have watched my dad paint with watercolours for years, and it has been incredibly rewarding to work with my family and see our passion for art and the medium grow into the Stoneground Paint Company." ✳

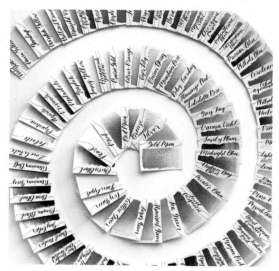

Quinacridone Violet

Hansa
Aureolin
Naples Yellow
Iso yellow
Hansa light + Aureolin
Hansa light + Naples Yellow
Hansa light + Iso Yellow
Qui
+ Hansa light + Aureolin + N
+ Iso Yellow
+ Quin Violet
Quin Violet
Hansa light + Aureolin + Naples yellow

"We've seen Stoneground watercolours used across continents and in many different countries, a variety of creative visions applied across platforms and mediums, and the unique artwork we've seen from around the world has been truly inspiring."

Stoneground Paint Company uses distilled water, honey and gum arabic to bind their pigment. "We are very aware of the critical role pollinators play in a healthy ecosystem. We source our honey through local beekeepers, often urban, and like to stay involved in the goings-on of the hives throughout the year. Bees, and other pollinators, are under threat around the world due to climate change, pesticide use and biodiversity loss, but even small actions such as growing flowers at home can help. Our own garden at home has been converted to a pollinator garden. And we encourage others to do the same."

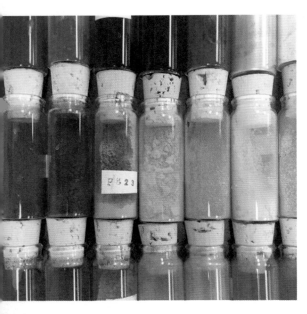

Making art supplies as they do at the Stoneground Paint Company is a slow, considered process. They use a variety of single pigment colours, some of which come directly from the rocks and soil that make up the earth around us. Many of their pigments are naturally occuring, known by artists as iron oxides, yellow ochres, siennas and umbers. Each pigment has a unique history—from the accidental discovery of Prussian blue (an 18th-century chemist, Heinrich Diesbach, was making some red pigment but had run out of a key ingredient: potash. He borrowed some from a friend who seems to have fobbed him off with potash contaminated with animal products. Overnight, Diesbach got a blue pigment instead of a red one), to the long and rich history of pigments like malachite (a bright green mineral) and azurite (a bright blue mineral) used by the Ancient Egyptians.

Once Stoneground has their pigment ready, they carefully mix pigment and binder (the binder for their watercolour paint is crafted by hand using distilled water, honey and gum arabic) with palette knives on large stone slabs. When combined (some pigments can take ages to mix, some take mere minutes), their paint-makers use hand-blown glass mullers to further grind and break up the pigment particles. This process is what makes handmade paint superior, as hand mulling breaks up pigment particles irregularly, which in turn scatters light in various ways, resulting in paint that is visually brighter to the human eye. The finished watercolour is then hand-poured. From start to finish, the entire process can take up to six weeks.

stonegroundpaint.com
@stonegroundpaintco

SUSAN GOODE

Susan Goode is a mosaic artist who makes everything from garden art and jewellery to furniture from upcycled and recycled materials. Full of tiny pieces of the past, her work is redolent of things that have been used and loved and then found a new life once again, in Susan's hands. The creations are inspired by early memories of her grandmother's home, where the shelves held ceramics and ornaments from the 1930s and 1940s, with their evocative patterns and colours. Susan grew up in the 1960s and 1970s, an era of bold patterns and colours in ceramics, too, although of a very different aesthetic than that seen on her grandmother's shelves: "I adore making colourful, interesting, useful pieces from unwanted, worn-out recycled items. I try to keep my designs sympathetic to, and in harmony with, the period and style."

Now in her sixties, Susan has been making since she was 10 years old. She learned to make through her own study and practice but has also taken many courses since studying art at school: "I've always loved the patterns of mosaic, and 30 years ago I did a one-day course with my daughter as a bonding day, which sparked the development of my own creations and going on to teach it." She now enables others, running workshops on how to make garden art and jewellery with broken china, and writing modules: "I am proud to have written many qualification modules for OCN (Open College Network) in mosaics and other art subjects so that other people could gain qualifications."

The journey from making art supplies to selling her own work and teaching has been personal

"I cut into the tableware saucers, plates, cups, ornaments, etc. I tend to cut the pieces with an artist's eye and try and save the designs or pieces that would be decorative and useable for artists to transform."

for Susan. She wanted to find a better work-life balance, to work less frantic hours: "Creating has always played a big part in supporting my mental wellbeing and nurturing my soul, as have teaching and showing others how to do this, too."

She runs Susan Goode Designs from her home in London. There, her garden and house are artistic workspaces, where she trims and cuts the ceramics using a tool called a "wheeled tile nipper," and sometimes uses a mini sander, too, when working outside in the garden is useful.

Susan's art supplies are vintage china, glass tesserae, alcohol inks, acrylic, pastels and mixed media. Her mosaics and jewellery are made using broken vintage ceramic tableware and constructed using a technique known as Picassiette, which translates as "stealing plates." "I like to use vintage crockery most of the time. I prefer bone china, as it is thinner and more decorative. But I also use more modern waste pieces sometimes, if the design is useful for textures." People often give her broken boxes of old ceramics or she will buy them from car boot sales, charity and antique shops. She will cut into the tableware saucers, plates, cups and ornaments, looking for a bit of pattern here, a colour there, already imagining what she will make with it.

"I am proud to be recycling and repurposing the crockery to stop it from going into landfills. What is the point of all the pieces of unwanted china when we can make wonderful new items to preserve the gorgeous heritage skills and patterns?"

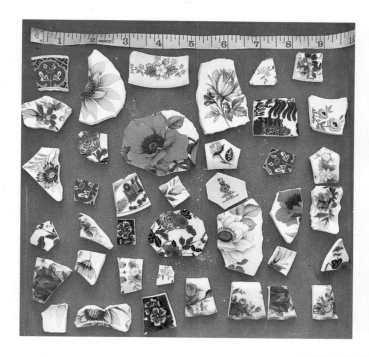

Her vintage ceramic art supplies, although abundant in her home country of England, are not always easy for others to source. When Susan realized that she had lots of pieces left over from her own projects, she wondered if they might be something other makers would be interested in buying and using, too. She began bagging up selections to sell: "to inspire others around the world to make and create from these little vintage delights. I realized some countries couldn't get the lovely vintage English ceramics we have and take for granted here in the UK, that English bone china could be a huge inspiration to makers who do not have that history of design in their own country." And indeed she found that customers love the chance to tap into her art supplies for making special pieces of art or jewellery themselves. ✳

PICASSIETTE

The mosaic word and tech-
nique Picassiette comes with
a lovely story. Raymond Isidore
(1900–1964), a graveyard
sweeper in Chartres, France,
in the first half of the 20th
century, decided to build his
own house and bought a plot
of land. Once it was finished
he decorated it, every inch,
with ceramic and glass mosaics set into cement. It took
him some 30 years to finish
it. Along the way Raymond
obsessively collected more
than 15 tons of broken plates
and cups for his project, so
locals nicknamed him "Picassiette," which translates as
"plate thief." A Picassiette or
trencadís (a Catalan term that
means "chopped") mosaic is
made from broken ceramic or
glass pieces cemented into a
base. The technique may have
been around for a long time,
used as a folk-art decoration,
but it gained fame through
the work of Catalan architect
Antoni Gaudí, who first used
it in the 1880s on his Güell
Pavilions complex in Spain.
Gaudí used discarded bits of
industrial ceramics found in
a tile factory and pieces of
white ceramic broken cups
and plates from others. Today
a Picassiette mosaic may also
include buttons, found objects
and jewellery.

TRACI BAUTISTA

Traci Bautista has been making art supplies, in one way or another, since she was eight years old—from handmade journals to carved stamps: "It's always been a part of my art-making process. I see the possibilities in everything."

"My creative path has been a winding road, from starting my career as a graphic designer working in Silicon Valley in the mid-1990s through the dot-com boom." She has worked as an event manager and a marketing exec, and moonlit as a professional XFL cheerleader. In 2001, she left a job in tech to work as a travelling K–12 art teacher in schools, art centres, nonprofit and after-school programs. She sold handmade journals and taught bookmaking. "Fast forward 20 years, I've travelled the world teaching in the US, Canada, Mexico, Bali and Australia. I launched an online education community in 2008. I blogged for 12 years and have written three best-selling mixed-media books. I'm working on my fourth book now! I design patterns for fabric and wallpaper, and licence my artwork for craft products, including stencils and stamps."

Over the past 10 years, Traci has made artisanal art supplies: watercolours, water media inks, clay paint, wax and encaustic crayons, botanical inks, paintbrushes, printmaking tools, and stamps and stencils. All of them are experimental and one-of-a-kind, swirling with personality and colour, like Traci herself. And all are handmade in California, in small batches, in limited quantities.

Traci attributes her infatuation with making paint to her friend, mixed-media artist Karen Michel,

"The act of creating art supplies is an art form of self-expression. It's a free-flowing journey into my creative practice and evolving intuitive, creative process."

who taught her how to make watercolours. "I was fascinated that I could turn turmeric into a beautiful golden yellow paint and charcoal into a shimmery black ink with gum arabic." Smitten with the process, Traci explored paint making, and in 2017, on a whim and a hashtag, launched #tracibautistaCOLOR in an Instagram post.

"I'd had much success throughout the years teaching and selling my handmade journals but I felt like I needed a shift in my artwork and creative business, so I decided to turn my love for paint making into a product and sell my handcrafted colours." Looking more like expensive chocolates (and just as addictive), her multicolour watercolours sell out quickly. Each pan is meticulously crafted, layer by layer: "They look like small abstract landscapes in a one-inch square pan, a little work of art."

"I share a piece of my creative spirit in each product I create," Traci says. Her botanical inks and foraged pigments have a connection to a specific place she has visited: "It's a deep spiritual journey that connects me to these materials. It's the adventure of hiking through the hills to find the beautiful cascading mountain of ochre rocks. It's the hunt for wild berries and yellow flowers of the acacia tree while strolling through an abandoned commune. It's on my daily walks with my pup, Indie, where I've foraged fallen eucalyptus leaves, rose mallow petals and tiny crepe myrtle flowers. Or in my backyard garden, where the coreopsis are turned into a gorgeous range of ink hues, from pinkish peach to brownish orange, to vibrant yellow."

Having a personal connection to her work is essential to Traci; it gives direct impetus for her colourful collections of paint. These are inspired by her everyday explorations, travels and love of colour: "Anything goes. The paints and journals I create are a collage, an expression of my creative journey at that moment of time in my life. Everything I make tells a story of memory or place." There is something so very

nice about buying art supplies made with such obsessive detail, personal passion and care. "There's a bohemian wanderlust vibe that resonates throughout," she says.

Inspiration for Traci's handcrafted paint begins in her sketchbook: "Even before a paint colour is created I choose a theme, take photos, brainstorm ideas, write and sketch to build a story around the collection. I create a collage of photos and colour swatches in Procreate—an inspiration board while I design a palette of paints." Then the meditative process of paint making begins. Pigments are placed on a marble slab, then mixed with a palette knife or metal scraper, then binder is drizzled from a mason jar: "Then it's a soulful dance as I move the glass muller in circles and a figure-eight motion." The pans are then hand poured, layer by layer, and topped off with metallic water media flakes. The pans are created over many days and will take up to a month to fully cure.

From there Traci's process is iterative: "Each paint is derived and designed around the first colour. One colour is created then slightly altered with additional pigments, and the dance repeats. As I make the paints, each colour is swatched in my paint recipe journals

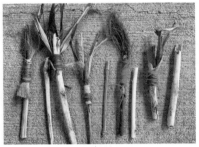

"My work and signature style has developed through the years. It has always been rooted in the foundation of a spirit of playfulness, colour, freedom and experimentation."

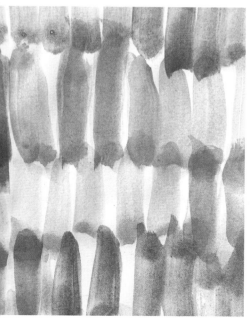

and tested on various paper substrates. I paint motifs to reflect the collection theme. These pieces are used to create a digital lookbook and in marketing." Traci has been pre-selling her paints from the beginning, which means she doesn't make more than she needs. She makes sure to create her products with sustainability in mind: "My paints and inks are presented in recyclable glass bottles adorned with hand-painted labels, and the watercolours are poured in metal pans. Once empty, both can be cleaned and refilled. Another sustainability consideration is my choice to create limited-edition collections in small batches. I acquire my pigments in small batches and often rotate colours once I have used up a pigment."

After more than two decades of being a creative artist-entrepreneur, Traci is as surprised as anyone how the art supplies have taken off: "I could never have imagined that an Instagram post would create an entirely new direction for my creative business. Thirty paint collections and 200-plus colours of inks and watercolours later, I *love* creating colourful products to encourage artists to play!" ✳

"For my handmade watercolours, I'm connected to the materials through the entire paint-making process of turning pigment into the final product: every step, from initial concept through gathering inspiration to physically mulling the paint to hand-pouring paint into bottles or pans. I touch everything. I share a piece of my creative spirit in each product I create."

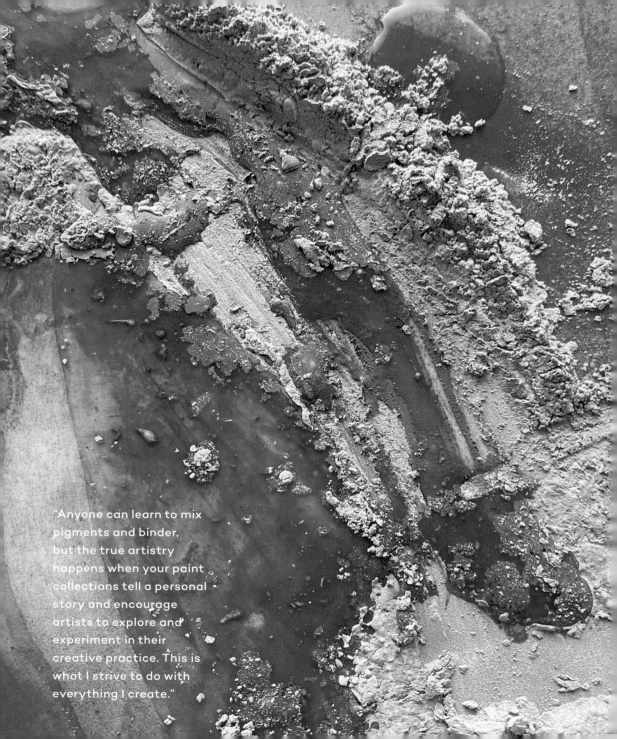

"Anyone can learn to mix pigments and binder, but the true artistry happens when your paint collections tell a personal story and encourage artists to explore and experiment in their creative practice. This is what I strive to do with everything I create."

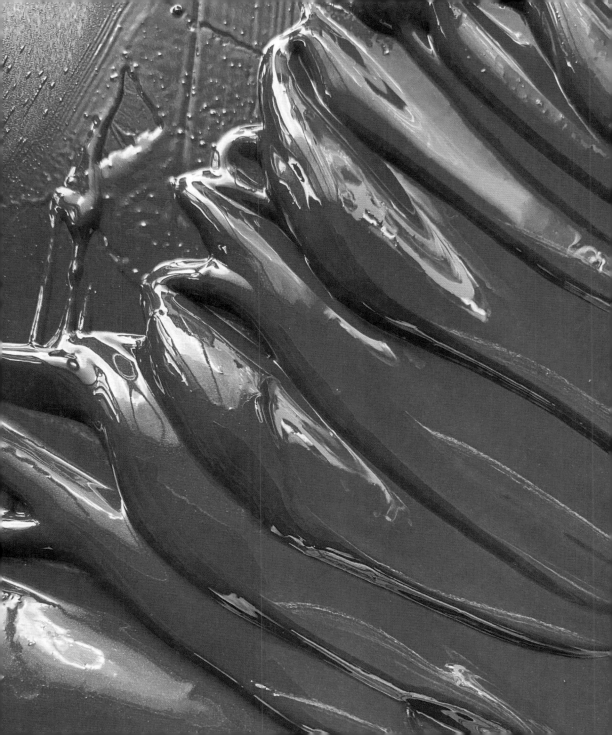

depending on the substrate, type of paper and the amount of water used when they are applied. The magic unfolds as the colours dry and the pigments start to separate. The colours have a lustre when light gently hits the surface and some have a slightly gritty texture."

Traci's Waxed Wedges, limited-edition encaustic paints, contain various waxes, damar resin (resin from an East Indian tree) and pigments. "Some have different variations of metallic sheen and multiple pigments and/or dyes. They can be used as a wax resist or heated and painted onto paper or canvas—perfect for your art journal or sketchbook."

Traci sources the raw material and pigments from online shops such as Sinopia, Earth Pigments, Natural Pigments and Kremer Pigments. "When I travel, I seek out art supply pigment shops. I've visited Maison Sennelier and Charvin in Paris. In Melbourne, Australia, I met master paint-maker David Coles and spent time talking about pigments and paint making in his shop, St. Luke Artist Colourman, and brought home a few pigments, including a jar of beautiful Australian ochre. For my botanical inks and paints, the items I forage are from my backyard garden and neighbourhood or found on hikes, and some natural dyes are purchased from Botanical Colors."

INGREDIENTS FOR ART-MAKING

The raw materials in Traci's watercolour paints include non-toxic inorganic (earth) and organic (modern) pigments and ethically sourced mica mixed with a custom mixed homemade binder (organic ingredients including gum arabic, local honey and clove oil).

Her handmade inks, such as the Kaleidoscope Florals artisan ink set, contain water-soluble dye and, occasionally, pigments. "The colours create a number of textured effects

CREATIVE SUSTAINABILITY

"One way I encourage my customers to incorporate sustainability into their art practice is to share ideas on how to reuse and recycle all of my product packaging," Traci says. "The cardboard boxes can become canvases with a little gesso painted on top, then adding collage and water. Those painted cardboard pieces can then be bound into a journal. All of the paint containers can be reused or refilled. The corrugated rolled packaging that covers the ink bottles can be reused and created into printmaking texture tools."

- Purchase supplies and materials from artists who create art materials with sustainability in mind.

- "Look with new eyes." There are so many possibilities in creating found tools and using things that are around your house, kitchen, garage or studio. Use old papers that can be painted over or cut up for collage. Turn packaging into canvases. Turn chopsticks, sticks or found objects into mark-making tools.

- Experiment with making botanical inks from local landscapes. Explore making paints with pigments of foraged rocks. Forage a small number of fallen leaves, rocks and florals a couple of times a year.

treicdesignsdigitals.com
@treicdesigns

"My botanical inks and foraged pigments have a connection to a specific place I have visited. It's a deep spiritual journey that connects me to these materials."

TYPOTHECARY INK

Megan Zettlemoyer makes inks with thoughtfully sourced and foraged materials including acorn caps, walnuts, poke-berries, avocado pits, flower petals, grapevines and cloves. Other ingredients include typical household goods like rubbing alcohol, baking soda, rusty objects and water. In her kitchen "lab," various combinations are cooked, mashed, ground, mixed, strained, filtered and shaken. The result of all this work is liquid inks, redolent of nature, with which Megan paints.

Trained as a graphic designer, Megan founded her own company, Typothecary Letterpress, in 2011. "After a few years of working for various in-house design agencies, I set out to find something more professionally and personally fulfilling." In 2019, whilst at a national letterpress conference, she stumbled upon an ink-making book. With that and her love of the outdoors, she started making inks from common plants and household products. This new direction pulled many things together for her: "My background in design contributes to the compositions whilst the chemical nature of the inks provides some beautiful surprises."

Initially, Megan hoped to make inks for letterpress printing but instead found she was able to use them in her own art: "I had the original hope of making ink for letterpress printing but quickly realized the inks I would actually be making would not be suitable for that use. Fortunately, that was not a deterrent and I was still thrilled with the idea that I could make my

"Being able to explore nature in its abundance while sustainably sampling its offerings to create these works has been an inspirational journey."

PORTRAIT BY SAM INTERRANTE

own colours! I wasn't necessarily looking to make art supplies but am always willing to try something new, especially when it combines multiple interests and art-making." She sells her paintings on her website, alongside prints, notecards and postcards—all posted out from Typothecary headquarters in Lancaster, Pennsylvania.

Her paintings are contained and a little bit chaotic at the same time: "The works I create tend to lean towards the abstract end of the spectrum while incorporating classic design principles. In most of my paintings, I pair a structured element with sporadic, energetic bursts which symbolize the balance of the serenity in nature with the often frenetic bustle of the city." Megan's colour palette is especially satisfying, with in-between, hard-to-pin-down colours. Her work is set apart by the translucency of her foraged inks—her paintings are a bit like tea stains, but from nature, as if the leaf or petal or nut had been imprinted, then removed. Megan doesn't sell her inks yet but enjoys seeing how other artists have used them.

In the end, for Megan, everything comes back to her first love of letterpress: "I love typography and the idea of incorporating characters as art, with more abstract design elements to play with them." She is constantly exploring how she can incorporate all her different art supplies and mediums together: "I am always exploring new combinations to expand my colour palette, which sparks new ideas and leads to various directions in imagery. Often, all it takes is providing someone with a fresh, 'new' art supply to unleash their creativity. We are all inherently creative beings, sometimes we just need a palette of pigments and some beautiful paper to unleash those innate abilities." ✳

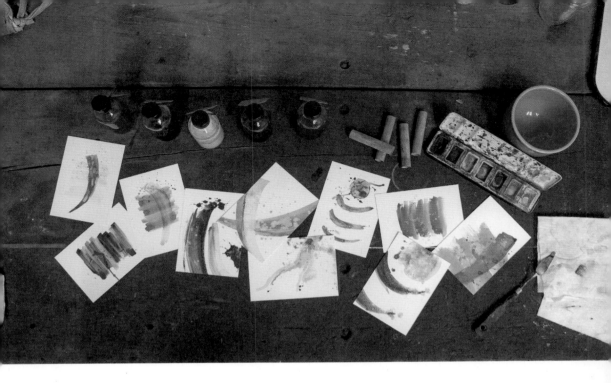

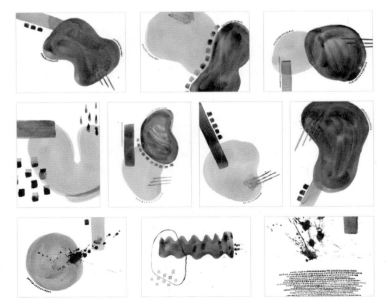

"When I am foraging materials I make sure to make mutually beneficial decisions such as sourcing small amounts from multiple plants and not removing more than the plant can tolerate to sustain itself. This way I'm able to return year after year to source my ingredients from the same locations."

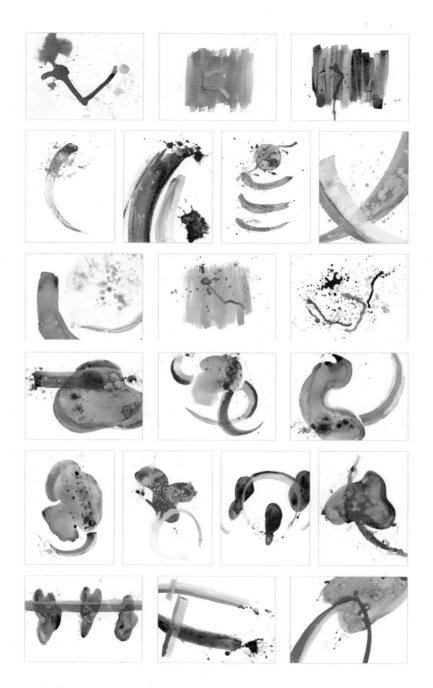

FRESH INK

The process of making each of Megan's inks starts with colour selection: "I have a wishlist of colours and each colour typically derives from certain seasonally available materials, so that will usually determine whether I'll be hiking in a forest or walking around town to source the raw materials. The best adventures include stumbling upon something unexpected that I can use to make a new colour."

Her kitchen area is her chemistry lab, where all the cooking, grinding and processing happens. All of her inks are bottled with anti-moulding agents to help with preservation. Some of the inks need to be refrigerated, while others can be stored at room temperature: "There is a minimal amount of chemistry equipment I use that is readily available from homebrewing or hobby shops. The processing of some of the natural materials does tend to leave permanent stains so I've given some old cookware a second lease on life for those duties!"

Because Megan's inks are created fresh and contain only natural preservatives, some of them have shown, over time, to alter in appearance when exposed to air and light: "As some of the raw ingredients are naturally acidic, it is possible that they could eventually break down the paper. All of these conditions are part of the ongoing exploration of the ink-making techniques and can be considered to be equally essential to creating each unique 'living' piece of art."

VIARCO

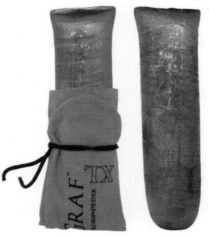

At the Viarco factory in São João da Madeira, Portugal, a singular huge red pencil hangs over the doorway—no other signage is needed. The Viarco art supplies brand has been around, in one form or another, since 1907, explains manager José Vieira: "The origin of pencil manufacture in Portugal dates back to 1907, when Conselheiro Figueiredo Faria, with his partner, the French engineer Jules Cacheux, decided to build an industrial unit for the manufacture of pencils in Vila do Conde. That brand was known as Portugália and it was the first pencil factory in Portugal." That company did not survive the Great Depression of 1929 to 1931. In 1930 it was bought by Manoel Vieira Araújo, a manufacturer of hats, who renamed it Viarco, after his hat factory. The company was managed by Manoel's son António. Ten years later the company was relocated in São João da Madeira, taking with it all the equipment and many employees, who decided to start a new life along with the factory. It is still there today.

The following years were marked by technological developments, a result of António's skills in mechanical engineering and product development. This led to the production of crayons and a wide range of technical pencils. Viarco became an iconic name for generations of Portuguese. José, the current manager, is the great-grandson of Manoel and has been at the helm of his family's business since 2000. "Since the 1930s a lot of things have happened: another world war, a dictatorship lasting over more than 40 years, a revolution, the European Union, the Internet and the

"Artists have always influenced and changed the world with their vision. Art give us the opportunity to see things that we never thought would exist. It allows us to see the future with just one look."

dream of a free world. Everything has changed except the Viarco factory."

The factory still makes pencils, of course, but the product range has expanded. For example, the ArtGraf Tailor Shape is a water-soluble pressed pigment block, inspired and shaped like traditional tailor's chalks. It can be used for drawing directly on a surface, or mixed with water to get a deep colour or a translucent one depending on how much liquid is added.

The idea for the Tailor Shape came from the artist Diogo Pimentão, during his residence at Viarco in 2008: "He showed me a drawing tool he had found whilst travelling," says José. "It was a small wheel and he explained to me that its different shape changed the way the body draws. The idea of a new shape started to become more concrete when we noticed that a lot of artists broke up their standard sticks of graphite or pastel before they started to work. We were searching for something that could be half of the size of a stick, and could provide a different approach to drawing." The shape of the ancient tailor chalk was perfect, because it gave them the functionality they were searching for, and at the same time was traditional and suited the old pencil factory.

ART GRAF

VIARCO TAILOR SHAPE
WATER-SOLUBLE

"Artists are the major influencers in the world and they should use their position to promote change, either by art or through their voice."

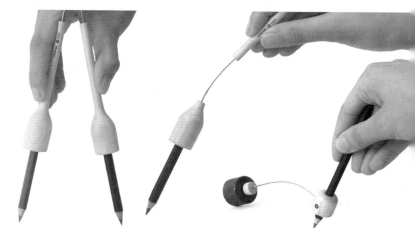

The Tailor Shapes are sold as individual tablets in earthy colours and primaries, and also come in charming cork palettes. They are manufactured in the same way as Viarco's graphite leads, but with different ingredients. For leads, clay and graphite are mixed, water is added and a lengthy blending begins. Water is then pressed out by running the mixture through compressor rolls before a second mixing happens. This creates a paste which is then extruded by forcing it through a thin tube to make pencil lead. Stamping the name on the Tailor Shape is the only difference. The first colour—black—was released in 2011, and in 2013 they released an earth tone set.

Viarco has long-term relationships with its main suppliers, preferring to source locally whenever possible. "We believe that our business should promote the development of our community. Nearly half of our raw materials are bought from Portuguese suppliers." The making of Viarco's products takes place in the historical surroundings of the original factory. Some processes are done by machine, some by hand: "The first process of any product is the mixing of the recipe. Each colour, each grade, has its own list of ingredients that are mixed with water, compressed, extruded and dried." The manufacturing facilities and some of the equipment are historical pieces dating from 1907.

A company with a long history, Viarco is part of the local creative community and attracts tourists as well. "We have an industrial tourism program and an atelier for artistic residences. Every year the factory runs exhibitions and events on illustration, poetry, music and art." Artist residencies benefit not only the artist, but also Viarco. "Each artist has their own language and personality; but they all share a curiosity about things and the capacity to play like children. Our product developments are the result of this collaboration." ❁

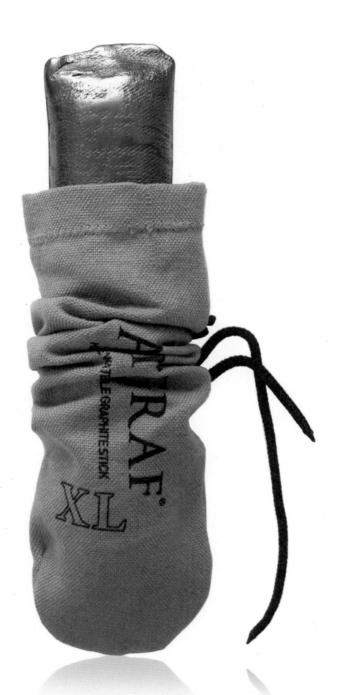

GRAPHITE XL

If size matters in your art supplies then the ArtGraf XL graphite stick is for you. Housed in a drawstring bag, this extra-large handmade, water-soluble stick made from German 8B graphite can be used for big artistic productions and large-scale drawings. The design of the ArtGraf XL was inspired by the artisanal processes used for the production of leads for Viarco pencils. A friend of José Vieira spotted the bags being used to dry the graphite, clay and water before it was used for making leads for pencils: "Isaque Pinheiro, a sculptor friend, told me during a visit to the factory that we should make a product based on that—something big to grab and texturize, inside a fabric bag, a small version of the originals in the factory."

viarco.pt
@viarcoportugal

WENDY BRIGHTBILL

Wendy Brightbill is in love with the process of painting: "Every time I pick up a paintbrush or a palette knife, I feel like I am speaking a hidden language—a language of beauty that cannot be communicated any other way." Wendy's mom was a maker and she grew up in a creative home; she remembers falling asleep to the whirring of the sewing machine in the next room. Wendy took several drawing courses in high school but never really enjoyed the process of making art. For her, it was always about getting to the finished piece, not about enjoying the process. She could copy a photograph in a pencil drawing, she remembers, but struggled to paint something from her imagination. That is, until a dramatic turning point: "It wasn't until a car accident rearranged my brain, that I started my creative journey. It was then that I found mixed-media art and fell in love with the process of making art." Her art practice became her therapy. It was this practice that helped her through several years of depression and trauma: "Over a decade later, I can't imagine my life without my creative practice. It has continued to help me heal and work through other traumas, including losing my mom to pancreatic cancer in 2020."

Wendy's paintings have a depth and visible roughness to the oil paint on the canvas—a technique known as impasto. "I would define my style as expressive impasto play. I love exploring texture, contrast and graphic shapes in my work. My work is playful, loose, abstracted and carefree." She mainly paints abstract

"I am always looking to create dimension through palette knife work and blending between colours. People often say that my work looks a lot like frosting on a cake."

"I want to encourage artists who are just beginning on their creative path. Don't be afraid to take more risks. Try a lot of different styles. Commit to your practice. Make art just for you."

florals, using a bright palette, and with relaxed compositions. She likes to add further depth to her oil paintings with collage: "I often am looking for ways to incorporate vintage elements into my artwork. I love perusing flea markets to find special things to incorporate into my work. I look for old fabrics, embroidered linens, lace and papers to use in my art. I also love incorporating these found elements into my art journaling practice as well. I find that using vintage collage in my work creates a story and history that you can't find anywhere else. I find so much beauty in old forgotten things."

Other inspirations are found in different ways. "I am often motivated by colour. In fact, colour is most often the starting point for all of my paintings. I find much of my colour inspiration from vintage colour palettes and Mother Nature. Colour truly is part of my therapy and often can change my mood in a matter of minutes." Wendy likes watching period cinema to gather inspiration for colour palettes and is also inspired by creating flower arrangements for her home: "I buy myself flowers on a regular basis, then take lots of photographs of the arrangements to use later as inspiration for my work. I follow floral designers and abstract painters online for that extra push into the studio."

After having worked as a kindergarten teacher, Wendy still loves teaching and sharing her passion and processes for art-making through her online courses. She wants to encourage artists who are just beginning on their creative path: "Don't be afraid to take more risks. Try a lot of different styles. Commit to your practice. Make art just for you." She has found that audiences are looking to connect with stories that they recognize, that strike a chord, that ring true: "I think what has helped me the most is showing up to my work, being vulnerable with my audience and telling my story. I have been surprised over the years by the amount of people who have found that my story and my work resonate with them. People are looking for authenticity. Art bridges the gap between people and communicates in a way when words fall flat. Art tells a story that can give people hope. Beauty brings healing." ✳

"I find that I make my best work when I paint just for myself. So while I sell a lot of my work, I always paint just for me and what I would want to hang in my own home."

SINGING
80
DANCING
90

A RECIPE FOR PAINTING

Wendy's favourite art medium is oil paint, straight out of the tube and onto her palette knife for her impasto work. She started using oil paint after running into limitations with acrylics several years ago. And she has never looked back: "There is a definite learning curve when learning how to use oil paint. But I love the luminosity and texture of oils. I often use cold wax medium to mix with oils to create textured layers for my paintings. I am always looking to create dimension through palette knife work and blending between colours."

Wendy's canvases are thick with oil paint, evocative of frosting on a cake. She enjoys building that texture in her work, she says: "But I like to switch up my process often, too, to keep things fresh. Sometimes I start my paintings with abstract work in acrylics and other mixed-media materials, like markers or gel pens. Then I will turn that abstract into a still-life painting by building with palette knife work, with oils and cold wax, over the abstract." She likes leaving parts of the abstract painting showing through to create depth and playfulness in the work. "I also love starting my florals with collaged fabrics and papers. Then, I layer cold wax medium over the top of the collage for an encaustic feel. Finally, I add the palette knife work with my oil paint on top of the cold wax."

wendybrightbill.com
@wendybrightbill

WINSOR & NEWTON

Winsor & Newton is one of the oldest names in the art supply world. Back in 1832, chemist William Winsor and artist Henry Newton brought together "the knowledge of the scientist, and the creativity of the artist to offer an unprecedented choice of colour, clarity and permanence to fine artists." The pair wanted to provide artists with consistent and reliable colours. First, they developed an improved range of watercolours. The moist, glycerine-based watercolours, designed especially for outdoor painting, came out in 1835. These were followed by a number of other innovations, including Chinese White, a durable opaque white watercolour in 1834 that remains their most popular white. In 1842 came collapsible tin tubes for oils and watercolours, to which Winsor & Newton added a patented screw top.

A series of royal appointments and awards in the late 1800s paved the way for Winsor & Newton to expand and take its colours around the world. The company was granted its first Royal Warrant by Queen Victoria in 1841. They remain by Appointment to HRH the Prince of Wales today and are able to display his coat of arms—three curly feathers—on their packaging. In the early 20th century, Winsor & Newton expanded its range to offer less expensive, more accessible art supplies. It also expanded its factories, ensuring that colour and brush production carried on through both world wars. Today a Winsor & Newton catalogue might include papers for all paints, markers, inks, canvases, brushes, tools, and watercolour,

"Our laboratory has two artists' studios next to it so that artists in residence can exchange ideas and experiences with our chemists, collaborating to develop perfect paintings and perfect materials. Artists are on our staff throughout the business, playing their part in technical, engineering and marketing departments."

oil, acrylic and gouache paint sets. But still, they are probably the name that comes to mind when people think of buying their first set of watercolours. Winsor & Newton are now part of the bigger art supply Colart family and have a head office in London.

Winsor & Newton produces 108 colours for their professional watercolours, more than enough to suit most artists' imaginations and needs. The paints are produced on custom-made machinery in their main factory in Le Mans, France. When Winsor & Newton first set out to make art supplies, all those years ago, artists including J. M. W. Turner (1775–1851) gave them advice. Turner was well known to be willing to try new art supplies. They now make a Turner's Yellow in his honour. Continuing to work with artists today, the company offers their Masterclass, a series of on-line professional learning tools for artists. Artists are part of Winsor & Newton's staff, too, working in the technical, engineering and marketing departments.

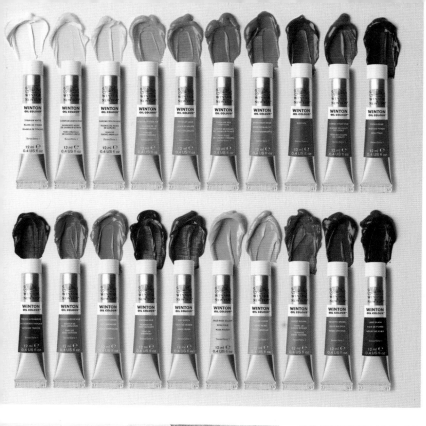

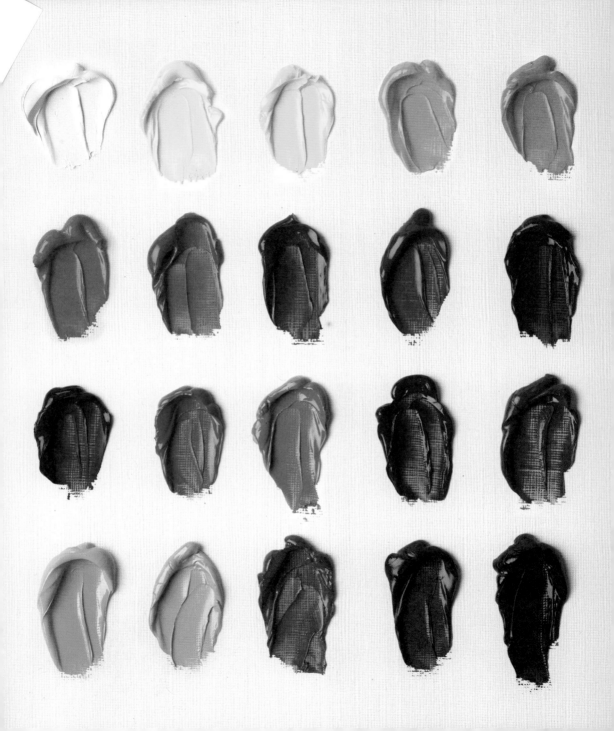

Despite manufacturing art supplies for over 170 years, some things have not changed. The original Winsor & Newton moist watercolours continue to be formulated and manufactured according to the founders' principles: "to create an unparalleled watercolour range which offers artists the widest and most balanced choice of pigments with the greatest possible permanence." But other things have changed. They continue to update and add to their ranges, keeping them relevant. It is lovely to see such an old and venerable art supply name as Winsor & Newton on the shelves of art supply shops still. Surely Mr. Turner would appreciate both the things that have stayed the same and the things that have improved in their art supplies since he shopped with them. ✳

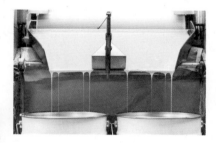

HOW TO MAKE A WATERCOLOUR

A Winsor & Newton Professional Watercolour pan is produced by combining a pigment with a binder (usually gum arabic). "There are two main processes involved: mixing the pigment and binder together and then milling this mix to super micron fineness," explains Winsor & Newton. Gum arabic "is colourless and does not compromise the natural character or colour of the pigments. Secondly, it is less soluble and provides stable adhesion of the colour upon the painting surface to enable the artist to apply layer upon layer of jewel-like colours without muddying the colours underneath. ... A variety of binders are manufactured to suit various pigments and each formulation contains a selection of these binders. ... Careful control of the milling process is essential, as it ensures a stable suspension of the pigment in the binder and helps release the full intensity of the colour. To make Professional Watercolour pans, each formulation has to undergo a further process. Generally, this involves a lengthy procedure of drying the colour and then extruding it into long sections. These are then cut into whole pan or half-pan sizes."

ZOË INGRAM

Zoë Ingram is an illustrator, an abstract artist, a designer and an author in Edinburgh, Scotland. Her illustration work is mainly for books and magazines, and is full of delicate patterns and simple but realistic figures. In her mixed-media abstract artwork—painted and collaged—realism is still present in a small way, but it is overlaid by marks and small blasts of colour; they are where her work has an altogether more dreamy aesthetic. Being able to offset the demands of commercial illustration by dedicating time to abstract art is essential for Zoë: "Making art makes me happy and at peace with myself, and it's important for me to have that to balance out the often demanding schedule within my illustration work. My illustration work is more often than not for a client, so painting is somewhere I can go to do whatever I please. I need the balance to keep me steady and fulfilled. I also like the challenge of trying to improve my skills and techniques. What I love about painting is that it enriches my illustration work and vice versa."

Zoë makes mixed-media paintings and collages, as well as digital compositions. "I love the beginning part of making a painting, the underpainting, and usually I begin by just drawing some expressive marks with a humble pencil," she describes. "The other tool that I love and is probably becoming a favourite is my iPad. It allows me to work quickly and try ideas out without the scariness of putting paint on a physical canvas, and it helps me improve my decision making when it comes to traditional painting."

"I can be inspired by the macro detail of a flower or signage on a shop front or a piece of music that moves me. I walk in nature for clarity and peace, and that inspires me. If I'm ever in an inspiration slump, I recognize that and get myself outside or visit an art exhibition."

Her collage process is fairly intuitive, too. She sifts through her collection of papers and plays around with the possibilities before sticking anything down: "I like to use contrasting patterns and textures. I will sometimes use traditional drawing or painting materials over the top of the papers that I stick down, to try to create more depth and differences in weight and interest points. I love to include floral elements and linear drawings over the top of my collages." She also sometimes mixes her paintings and collages: "I love the clean lines when I make collage but I'm equally in love with the wild and free expression of paint. A combination of the two is beautiful."

Zoë studied textiles at college, and then worked in a design and advertising agency for a decade, learning all sorts of useful techniques that would come into their own later on, like scanning, making mock-ups and cutting objects out in Photoshop. She uses all sorts of art supplies, from acrylic inks to the "humble pencil." And as far as tools are concerned, anything goes. She is even known to use an old credit card for mark making. When she is working in mixed media (especially in her sketchbook explorations) she will grab whatever she feels is needed to add interest to the piece: "I'll usually start with some thinner layers of watery paint and then perhaps add some watercolour pencil or ink pencil lines, which can be very vibrant. The interaction with the pencil

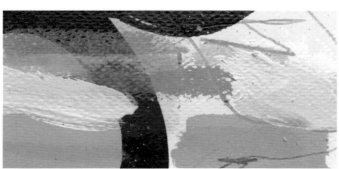

on the wet paint creates some unexpected results. The element of surprise is fun. I will then continue building, using everything from basic pencil to acrylic paint, collage, oil pastel, gouache and acrylic inks, which are really fun to use as drips or with a dip pen."

As a self-confessed dreamy introvert and INFP personality (meaning she has introverted, intuitive, feeling and prospecting personality traits), Zoë can easily be engrossed at any moment by her louder inner life: "My motivation when it comes to painting, you could say, is very selfish really. But I think of it as self-care. I do it for me and if anyone else likes it then that's a bonus." She began to paint as a way to express her feelings and process her emotions after her husband passed in 2018. "What I make is both a form of communication and a part of me. I love the injection of meaning in my work, and, being fairly introverted, with art I can put myself out there, where the art is the focus instead of me." ✳

INTUITIVE EXPRESSION

"I use a wide variety of media and often jump between traditional and digital applications," Zoë says of her art supplies. "Gouache is my main paint of choice for illustration and I also use it when I'm painting abstracts or if I'm painting my own papers for collage. For my personal art practice, though, anything goes: acrylic ink, acrylic paint, acrylic gouache, pencil, wax crayon, oil pastel, biro pens, watercolour and ink pencils, paint pens and markers. With mark making, I have a bunch of brushes, an old credit card for spreading and moving paint, and my dip pen, which I love."

Whether working digital or not, Zoë starts off slowly: "I always begin by just making some random expressive marks on the page or canvas. I then build layers using thinner paint at first, building up to thicker marks." A lot of her abstract work includes some black to anchor the view, as well as a small, realistic element, such as a leaf or an animal. And then she lets go with her colours: "I love the play between colours, the contrast between heavy and light lines, the juxtaposition between something tight and something messy." She is used to listening to her feelings when working, with each work telling her what to do next: "The composition usually happens organically throughout the process, and the piece that I'm working on tells me what to do next. It's a very intuitive process and is never premeditated. I never have a solid plan before I begin and that's part of the appeal for me. It's always a surprise when a painting is finished."

zoeingram.com
@_zoeingram_

JANE AUDAS

A writer, journalist, curator and museum professional, Jane Audas has written for magazines such as *World of Interiors, Arts Society Magazine, Vogue Japan, Crafts, Embroidery* and *HALI*, and is a core contributor to UPPERCASE. She has also contributed essays to several books on craft and design. Jane curated several exhibitions of contemporary craft including *W Is for Wallpaper* and *Under Your Feet: The Contemporary Rug* at Ruthin Craft Centre, Wales. She studied design history all the way up to an MPhil at the Royal College of Art, where she specialized in the history of shops and shop display. Jane has also spent many years making digital things happen in exhibitions and on websites for museums like the V&A, Science Museum and Natural History Museum in London. ✳

janeaudas.com
@janeaudas

ENCYCLOPEDIA
OF
INSPIRATION

UPPERCASE

A multi-volume book series released in whimsical (non-alphabetical) order on all manner of intriguing and creative topics.

@uppercasemag
uppercasemagazine.com

encyclopediaofinspiration.com